Ninja Dual Zone

Air Fryer

Cookbook

UK 2023

1000 Days Foolproof and Crispy Recipes for Your Whole Family to Master

Double Zone Air Fryer

Kacey Botsford

Warning-Disclaimer

The purpose of this book is to educate and entertain. The author or publisher does not guarantee that anyone following the techniques, suggestions, tips, ideas, or strategies will become successful. The author and publisher shall have neither liability or responsibility to anyone with respect to any loss or damage caused, or alleged to be caused, directly or indirectly by the information contained in this book.

Table of Contents

Chapter 7 Holiday Specials   49

Chapter 8 Desserts   54

INTRODUCTION

Like most cooks, I love the air fryer. It's easy to take a portion of food and make it crispy and delicious when you own one. So, of course, many air fryers are on the market nowadays. To make things more confusing, each offers buzzword-laden features that are supposed to wow the buyer. This book will look at the Ninja Foodi Dual Zone Air Fryer.

I love Ninja's air fryer. Before I bought this, I was annoyed with how little food my previous air fryer could cook. I have a family to feed, and kids grow impatient when you can only cook one serving at a time. The air fryer I owned last couldn't do much beyond making food crisp.

This air fryer offers so much more, which makes sense. So many are looking for an all-in-one appliance that isn't a jack-of-all-trades, and Ninja's air fryer not only lets you do a lot but lets you do it well.

When I decided to buy this air fryer, I went from ordering fast food half the time to cooking exclusively at home. At around $200, this air fryer is a small price to pay for how much you'll save as you cook from home. Unfortunately, with things costing more and more, we have to cut corners with spending. However, with this air fryer, you can save good food when you cut your food costs.

Because I've been cooking more, I've been making my own recipes using my Ninja Foodi. Some recipes I've come up with on my own, while others are my take on classic recipes. Either way, you'll find these recipes to be filling, easy to make, and, best of all, delicious. If you're new to the cooking world, no worries. I've made these recipes as easy to follow as possible. Trust me; I'm bad at following directions, so I made it easy for people of all skill levels.

Here's hoping that you enjoy my book. I'll examine why the Ninja Foodi Dual Zone Air Fryer is a good pick. With so many air fryers to choose from, why pick this one? I'll explain. Without further ado, let's begin.

Chapter 1: Getting to know the Ninja Foodi Dual Zone Air Fryer

Ninja introduced their Foodi lineup of air fryers in 2018, and since then, they've created several iterations of them in the years that have followed. The Dual Zone model, which I'll be discussing in this chapter, was released in 2022 and has received positive reviews from most people who have purchased it. Many reviewers say that this is the one if you need an appliance that does it all. But why is this air fryer so popular? To know this, we must first know how it works. So let's look at this.

How Does Ninja Foodi Dual Zone Air Fryer Work?

While people call it an air fryer, this device combines the air fryer and the pressure cooker. Therefore, to know how this device works, we must look at how these appliances operate.

An air fryer circulates hot air at high speed, which cooks food evenly to achieve a deep-fried state without needing oil. While similar to a convection oven, many people love deep fryers for how fast and small they cook.

Meanwhile, a pressure cooker cooks food through steam under high pressure. When you cook foods this way, you can get quick results, though pressure cooking does require water for it to work. Pressure cookers have been a popular way to cook food far longer than air fryers, though modern pressure cookers allow you to cook safer and more accessible than ever before.

The Ninja Foodi also works through two separate drawers. With these drawers, you can cook two types of food relatively quickly, something traditional air fryers do not offer.

Now, let's dive into the features of the Ninja Foodi Dual Zone Air Fryer. This air fryer packs quite a bit.

4 Top Features of Ninja Foodi Dual Zone Air Fryer

2 Independent Drawers

Again, one painful feature of the traditional air fryer is that you can cook only one serving at a time. This air fryer makes cooking faster by giving you two drawers. Not only that, these drawers are independent. They can be cooked differently, which is great if you're trying to cook two different foods that may require different settings.

Smart Finish & Match Cook

When you cook, you can choose between either of these options. Is it a marketing gimmick? On the contrary, it's an elegant feature. For example, if you choose Smart Finish, you can cook two different foods in two ways but program them so that both are done simultaneously. So you don't have to wait for one type of food to finish while the other gets cold.

With Match Cook, you can copy the settings for both drawers. This works well if you're cooking the same type of food.

So as you can see, both have their purpose.

6-in-1 Functionality

The Ninja Foodi combines an air fryer with an Instant Pot, giving you six ways to cook. You can air fry, air broil, roast, bake, reheat, or dehydrate your foods. You may not use all six functions, but I have used all six at least once. Sometimes, you want to cook some leftovers, you know?

Oversized Capacity

You want to cook for your family (or maybe you're starving), and the regular air fryer isn't cutting it. This air fryer can cook 8 quarts or up to 4 lbs. It's easy to cook for everyone quickly, meaning you don't need to cook multiple batches in the air fryer for an impatient family!

Ninja Foodi Dual Zone Air Fryer Cooking Tips

- ♦ First, read the manual. The manual is informative, providing some excellent tips with colorful illustrations.
- ♦ With any air fryer, shake the drawer halfway through, or turn the food manually to ensure even coating.
- ♦ Be sure to put the crisper tray at the bottom. This tray promotes even browning, making your foods delicious!
- ♦ Preheat the air fryer for a few minutes. While it's not mandatory, it helps ensure you're getting consistent cooking.
- ♦ An air fryer allows you to check on your food periodically without losing heat. So be sure to check it often!
- ♦ Avoid using aerosol cooking sprays, as these can be difficult to clean. Instead, brush your food with oil if you want to add a bit to make it crispy.
- ♦ Clean your drawers and crisper plates periodically. The drawers and crisper plates are easy to clean by hand, but you can also pop them in the dishwasher. Too much residue can impede cooking or cause your foods to smoke, and no one wants that!
- ♦ Use the appropriate settings depending on what you're cooking. These recipes will tell you what settings you should choose for your cooking.

Frequently Asked Questions

What's the Difference Between This and the Walmart Version?

The Walmart version is cheaper, but it has only four functions: Air fry, roast, reheat, and dehydrate. If that's good enough, you may prefer that version, but I like more variety.

Is it Possible to Bake a Cake in This?

Yes! This air fryer does have a bake option, which you can use to bake tiny cakes. I love that I can cook smaller, guilt-free cakes that don't have too many calories yet are rich and filling.

What Accessories Does This Air Fryer Have?

On Ninja's website, you can find a double-stack rack for air frying and a broiler rack. I like that it only has a few extra accessories. Too many, and it can get a little confusing!

Is it Possible to Go Over 400 Degrees F?

Only in broil mode. On the other modes, 400 is the limit. With that said, that's all you need to create some delicious air-fried food.

Are There Any Preset Buttons?

If you're looking for buttons such as "pizza," "veggies," etc., this air fryer does not have them. However, it has a cheat sheet that tells you the ideal settings. Remember, your results can vary, so use that as a springboard to find the best time that works for you.

Does It Use a Lot of Electricity?

Being smaller, the Ninja can be an excellent alternative to the oven. While I did not notice my bills lowering drastically, they did not go up. The Ninja is reasonably economical when it comes to power usage.

Care and Cleaning

♦ Clean often. If substances are stuck on the Ninja, cleaning them sooner or later can save you some headaches.

♦ Remember, the drawer and racks are machine washable, so popping them in the dishwasher can save you some headaches when all else fails. That said, hand washing the drawer can extend its lifespan, depending on your dishwasher and how gentle it is with cleaning.

♦ Wipe down the air fryer with a damp cloth every so often, particularly if food gets on it.

♦ Never immerse the air fryer outside the drawers and racks in water. You should know why.

♦ When wiping it down, be sure that you unplug before doing so.

♦ If there's food stuck in the drawer, submerge it in warm, soapy water for an hour or two.

Chapter 2 Breakfasts

Chapter 2 Breakfasts

Breakfast Meatballs

Prep time: 10 minutes | Cook time: 15 minutes | Makes 18 meatballs

450 g pork sausage meat, removed from casings
½ teaspoon salt
¼ teaspoon ground black pepper

120 ml shredded sharp Cheddar cheese
30 g cream cheese, softened
1 large egg, whisked

1. Combine all ingredients in a large bowl. Form mixture into eighteen 1-inch meatballs. 2. Place meatballs into the two ungreased air fryer drawers. Adjust the temperature to 204ºC and air fry for 15 minutes, shaking drawers three times during cooking. Meatballs will be browned on the outside and have an internal temperature of at least 64ºC when completely cooked. Serve warm.

Breakfast Calzone and Western Frittata

Prep time: 25 minutes | Cook time: 20 minutes | Serves 5

Breakfast Calzone:
350 ml shredded Mozzarella cheese
120 ml blanched finely ground almond flour
30 g full-fat cream cheese
1 large whole egg
4 large eggs, scrambled
230 g cooked sausage meat, removed from casings and crumbled
8 tablespoons shredded mild Cheddar cheese

Western Frittata:
½ red or green pepper, cut into ½-inch chunks
1 teaspoon olive oil
3 eggs, beaten
60 ml grated Cheddar cheese
60 ml diced cooked ham
Salt and freshly ground black pepper, to taste
1 teaspoon butter
1 teaspoon chopped fresh parsley

Make the Breakfast Calzone (zone 1 drawer): 1. In a large microwave-safe bowl, add Mozzarella, almond flour, and cream cheese. Microwave for 1 minute. Stir until the mixture is smooth and forms a ball. Add the egg and stir until dough forms. 2. Place dough between two sheets of parchment and roll out to ¼-inch thickness. Cut the dough into four rectangles. 3. Mix scrambled eggs and cooked sausage together in a large bowl. Divide the mixture evenly among each piece of dough, placing it on the lower half of the rectangle. Sprinkle each with 2 tablespoons Cheddar. 4. Fold over the rectangle to cover the egg and meat mixture. Pinch, roll, or use a wet fork to close the edges completely. 5. Cut a piece of parchment to fit your air fryer drawer and place the calzones onto the parchment. Place parchment into the zone 1 air fryer drawer. 6. Adjust the temperature to 192ºC and air fry for 15 minutes. 7. Flip the calzones halfway through the cooking time. When done, calzones should be golden in color. Serve immediately.

Make the Western Frittata (zone 2 drawer): 1. Preheat the zone 2 air fryer drawer to 204ºC. 2. Toss the peppers with the olive oil and air fry for 6 minutes, shaking the drawer once or twice during the cooking process to redistribute the ingredients. 3. While the vegetables are cooking, beat the eggs well in a bowl, stir in the Cheddar cheese and ham, and season with salt and freshly ground black pepper. Add the air-fried peppers to this bowl when they have finished cooking. 4. Place a cake pan into the zone 2 air fryer drawer with the butter, using an aluminum sling to lower the pan into the drawer. Air fry for 1 minute at 192ºC to melt the butter. Remove the cake pan and rotate the pan to distribute the butter and grease the pan. Pour the egg mixture into the cake pan and return the pan to the air fryer, using the aluminum sling. 5. Air fry at 192ºC for 12 minutes, or until the frittata has puffed up and is lightly browned. Let the frittata sit in the air fryer for 5 minutes to cool to an edible temperature and set up. Remove the cake pan from the air fryer, sprinkle with parsley and serve immediately.

Spinach and Swiss Frittata with Mushrooms

Prep time: 10 minutes | Cook time: 20 minutes | Serves 4

Olive oil cooking spray
8 large eggs
½ teaspoon salt
½ teaspoon black pepper
1 garlic clove, minced
475 ml fresh baby spinach

110 g baby mushrooms, sliced
1 shallot, diced
120 ml shredded Swiss cheese, divided
Hot sauce, for serving (optional)

1. Preheat the air fryer to 182ºC. Lightly coat the inside of a 6-inch round cake pan with olive oil cooking spray. 2. In a large bowl, beat the eggs, salt, pepper, and garlic for 1 to 2 minutes, or until well combined. 3. Fold in the spinach, mushrooms, shallot, and 60 ml the Swiss cheese. 4. Pour the egg mixture into the prepared cake pan, and sprinkle the remaining 60 ml Swiss over the top. 5. Place into the zone 1 air fryer drawer and bake for 18 to 20 minutes, or until the eggs are set in the center. 6. Remove from the air fryer and allow to cool for 5 minutes. Drizzle with hot sauce (if using) before serving.

Breakfast Sammies

Prep time: 15 minutes | Cook time: 20 minutes | Serves 5

Biscuits:
6 large egg whites
475 ml blanched almond flour, plus more if needed
1½ teaspoons baking powder
½ teaspoon fine sea salt
60 ml (½ stick) very cold unsalted butter (or lard for dairy-free), cut into ¼-inch

pieces
Eggs:
5 large eggs
½ teaspoon fine sea salt
¼ teaspoon ground black pepper
5 (30 g) slices Cheddar cheese (omit for dairy-free)
10 thin slices ham

1. Spray the two air fryer drawers with avocado oil. Preheat the air fryer to 176°C. Grease two pie pans or two baking pans that will fit inside your air fryer. 2. Make the biscuits: In a medium-sized bowl, whip the egg whites with a hand mixer until very stiff. Set aside. 3. In a separate medium-sized bowl, stir together the almond flour, baking powder, and salt until well combined. Cut in the butter. Gently fold the flour mixture into the egg whites with a rubber spatula. If the dough is too wet to form into mounds, add a few tablespoons of almond flour until the dough holds together well. 4. Using a large spoon, divide the dough into 5 equal portions and drop them about 1 inch apart on one of the greased pie pans. Place the pan in the two air fryer drawers and bake for 11 to 14 minutes, until the biscuits are golden brown. Remove from the air fryer and set aside to cool. 5. Make the eggs: Set the air fryer to 192°C. Crack the eggs into the remaining greased pie pan and sprinkle with the salt and pepper. Place the eggs in the air fryer to bake for 5 minutes, or until they are cooked to your liking. 6. Open the air fryer and top each egg yolk with a slice of cheese (if using). Bake for another minute, or until the cheese is melted. 7. Once the biscuits are cool, slice them in half lengthwise. Place 1 cooked egg topped with cheese and 2 slices of ham in each biscuit. 8. Store leftover biscuits, eggs, and ham in separate airtight containers in the fridge for up to 3 days. Reheat the biscuits and eggs on a baking sheet in a preheated 176°C air fryer for 5 minutes, or until warmed through.

Mexican Breakfast Pepper Rings

Prep time: 5 minutes | Cook time: 10 minutes | Serves 4

Olive oil
1 large red, yellow, or orange pepper, cut into four ¾-inch rings

4 eggs
Salt and freshly ground black pepper, to taste
2 teaspoons salsa

1. Preheat the air fryer to 176°C. Lightly spray two baking pans with olive oil. 2. Place 4 bell pepper rings on the two pans. Crack one egg into each bell pepper ring. Season with salt and black pepper. 3. Spoon ½ teaspoon of salsa on top of each egg. 4. Place the two pans in the two air fryer drawers. Air fry until the yolk is slightly runny, 5 to 6 minutes or until the yolk is fully cooked, 8 to 10 minutes. 5. Serve hot.

Homemade Toaster Pastries

Prep time: 10 minutes | Cook time: 11 minutes | Makes 6 pastries

Oil, for spraying
1 (425 g) package refrigerated piecrust
6 tablespoons jam or preserves of choice

475 ml icing sugar
3 tablespoons milk
1 to 2 tablespoons sprinkles of choice

1. Preheat the air fryer to 176°C. Line the zone 1 air fryer drawer with parchment and spray lightly with oil. 2. Cut the piecrust into 12 rectangles, about 3 by 4 inches each. You will need to reroll the dough scraps to get 12 rectangles. 3. Spread 1 tablespoon of jam in the center of 6 rectangles, leaving ¼ inch around the edges. 4. Pour some water into a small bowl. Use your finger to moisten the edge of each rectangle. 5. Top each rectangle with another and use your fingers to press around the edges. Using the tines of a fork, seal the edges of the dough and poke a few holes in the top of each one. Place the pastries in the prepared drawer. 6. Air fry for 11 minutes. Let cool completely. 7. In a medium bowl, whisk together the icing sugar and milk. Spread the icing over the tops of the pastries and add sprinkles. Serve immediately.

Jalapeño Popper Egg Cups and Cheddar Soufflés

Prep time: 25 minutes | Cook time: 12 minutes | Serves 6

Jalapeño Popper Egg Cups:
4 large eggs
60 ml chopped pickled jalapeños
60 g full-fat cream cheese
120 ml shredded sharp Cheddar cheese

Cheddar Soufflés:
3 large eggs, whites and yolks separated
¼ teaspoon cream of tartar
120 ml shredded sharp Cheddar cheese
85 g cream cheese, softened

Make the Jalapeño Popper Egg Cups (zone 1 drawer): 1. In a medium bowl, beat the eggs, then pour into four silicone muffin cups. 2. In a large microwave-safe bowl, place jalapeños, cream cheese, and Cheddar. Microwave for 30 seconds and stir. Take a spoonful, approximately ¼ of the mixture, and place it in the center of one of the egg cups. Repeat with remaining mixture. 3. Place egg cups into the zone 1 air fryer drawer. 4. Adjust the temperature to 160°C and bake for 10 minutes. 5. Serve warm.

Make the Cheddar Soufflés (zone 2 drawer): 1. In a large bowl, beat egg whites together with cream of tartar until soft peaks form, about 2 minutes. 2. In a separate medium bowl, beat egg yolks, Cheddar, and cream cheese together until frothy, about 1 minute. Add egg yolk mixture to whites, gently folding until combined. 3. Pour mixture evenly into four ramekins greased with cooking spray. Place ramekins into the zone 2 air fryer drawer. Adjust the temperature to 176°C and bake for 12 minutes. Eggs will be browned on the top and firm in the center when done. Serve warm.

Sausage and Cheese Balls

Prep time: 10 minutes | Cook time: 12 minutes |

Makes 16 balls

450 g pork sausage meat, removed from casings	30 g full-fat cream cheese, softened
120 ml shredded Cheddar cheese	1 large egg

1. Mix all ingredients in a large bowl. Form into sixteen (1-inch) balls. Place the balls into the two air fryer drawers. 2. Adjust the temperature to 204ºC and air fry for 12 minutes. 3. Shake the drawers two or three times during cooking. Sausage balls will be browned on the outside and have an internal temperature of at least 64ºC when completely cooked. 4. Serve warm.

Asparagus and Bell Pepper Strata and Greek Bagels

Prep time: 20 minutes | Cook time: 14 to 20 minutes

| Serves 6

Asparagus and Bell Pepper Strata:	½ teaspoon dried thyme
8 large asparagus spears, trimmed and cut into 2-inch pieces	Greek Bagels:
	120 ml self-raising flour, plus more for dusting
80 ml shredded carrot	120 ml plain Greek yoghurt
120 ml chopped red pepper	1 egg
2 slices wholemeal bread, cut into ½-inch cubes	1 tablespoon water
	4 teaspoons sesame seeds or za'atar
3 egg whites	Cooking oil spray
1 egg	1 tablespoon butter, melted
3 tablespoons 1% milk	

Make the Asparagus and Bell Pepper Strata (zone 1 drawer): 1. In a baking pan, combine the asparagus, carrot, red bell pepper, and 1 tablespoon of water. Bake in the air fryer at 166ºC for 3 to 5 minutes, or until crisp-tender. Drain well. 2. Add the bread cubes to the vegetables and gently toss. 3. In a medium bowl, whisk the egg whites, egg, milk, and thyme until frothy. 4. Pour the egg mixture into the pan. Bake in the zone 1 drawer for 11 to 15 minutes, or until the strata is slightly puffy and set and the top starts to brown. Serve.

Make the Greek Bagels (zone 2 drawer): 1. In a large bowl, using a wooden spoon, stir together the flour and yoghurt until a tacky dough forms. Transfer the dough to a lightly floured work surface and roll the dough into a ball. 2. Cut the dough into 2 pieces and roll each piece into a log. Form each log into a bagel shape, pinching the ends together. 3. In a small bowl, whisk the egg and water. Brush the egg wash on the bagels. 4. Sprinkle 2 teaspoons of the toppings on each bagel and gently press it into the dough. 5. Insert the crisper plate into the zone 2 drawer and the drawer into the unit.

Preheat the drawer by selecting BAKE, setting the temperature to 166ºC, and setting the time to 3 minutes. Select START/STOP to begin. 6. Once the drawer is preheated, spray the crisper plate with cooking spray. Drizzle the bagels with the butter and place them into the drawer. 7. Select BAKE, set the temperature to 166ºC, and set the time to 10 minutes. Select START/STOP to begin. 8. When the cooking is complete, the bagels should be lightly golden on the outside. Serve warm.

Potatoes Lyonnaise

Prep time: 10 minutes | Cook time: 31 minutes | Serves 4

1 sweet/mild onion, sliced	thick
1 teaspoon butter, melted	1 tablespoon vegetable oil
1 teaspoon brown sugar	Salt and freshly ground black pepper, to taste
2 large white potatoes (about 450 g in total), sliced ½-inch	

1. Preheat the air fryer to 188ºC. 2. Toss the sliced onions, melted butter and brown sugar together in the zone 1 air fryer drawer. Air fry for 8 minutes, shaking the drawer occasionally to help the onions cook evenly. 3. While the onions are cooking, bring a saucepan of salted water to a boil on the stovetop. Par-cook the potatoes in boiling water for 3 minutes. Drain the potatoes and pat them dry with a clean kitchen towel. 4. Add the potatoes to the onions in the zone 1 air fryer drawer and drizzle with vegetable oil. Toss to coat the potatoes with the oil and season with salt and freshly ground black pepper. 5. Increase the air fryer temperature to 204ºC and air fry for 20 minutes, tossing the vegetables a few times during the cooking time to help the potatoes brown evenly. 6. Season with salt and freshly ground black pepper and serve warm.

Cheddar-Ham-Corn Muffins

Prep time: 10 minutes | Cook time: 6 to 8 minutes |

Makes 8 muffins

180 ml cornmeal/polenta	120 ml shredded sharp Cheddar cheese
60 ml flour	
1½ teaspoons baking powder	120 ml diced ham
¼ teaspoon salt	8 foil muffin cups, liners removed and sprayed with cooking spray
1 egg, beaten	
2 tablespoons rapeseed oil	
120 ml milk	

1. Preheat the air fryer to 200ºC. 2. In a medium bowl, stir together the cornmeal, flour, baking powder, and salt. 3. Add egg, oil, and milk to dry ingredients and mix well. 4. Stir in shredded cheese and diced ham. 5. Divide batter among the muffin cups. 6. Place filled muffin cups in two air fryer drawers and bake for 5 minutes. 7. Reduce temperature to 166ºC and bake for 1 to 2 minutes or until toothpick inserted in center of muffin comes out clean.

Lemon-Blueberry Muffins

Prep time: 5 minutes | Cook time: 20 to 25 minutes |
Makes 6 muffins

300 ml almond flour
3 tablespoons granulated
sweetener
1 teaspoon baking powder
2 large eggs

3 tablespoons melted butter
1 tablespoon almond milk
1 tablespoon fresh lemon juice
120 ml fresh blueberries

1. Preheat the zone 1 air fryer drawer to 176°C. Lightly coat 6 silicone muffin cups with vegetable oil. Set aside. 2. In a large mixing bowl, combine the almond flour, sweetener, and baking soda. Set aside. 3. In a separate small bowl, whisk together the eggs, butter, milk, and lemon juice. Add the egg mixture to the flour mixture and stir until just combined. Fold in the blueberries and let the batter sit for 5 minutes. 4. Spoon the muffin batter into the muffin cups, about two-thirds full. Air fry in the zone 1 drawer for 20 to 25 minutes, or until a toothpick inserted into the center of a muffin comes out clean. 5. Remove the drawer from the air fryer and let the muffins cool for about 5 minutes before transferring them to a wire rack to cool completely.

Sausage and Egg Breakfast Burrito

Prep time: 5 minutes | Cook time: 30 minutes | Serves 6

6 eggs
Salt and pepper, to taste
Cooking oil
120 ml chopped red pepper
120 ml chopped green pepper
230 g chicken sausage meat

(removed from casings)
120 ml salsa
6 medium (8-inch) flour tortillas
120 ml shredded Cheddar
cheese

1. In a medium bowl, whisk the eggs. Add salt and pepper to taste. 2. Place a skillet on medium-high heat. Spray with cooking oil. Add the eggs. Scramble for 2 to 3 minutes, until the eggs are fluffy. Remove the eggs from the skillet and set aside. 3. If needed, spray the skillet with more oil. Add the chopped red and green bell peppers. Cook for 2 to 3 minutes, until the peppers are soft. 4. Add the sausage meat to the skillet. Break the sausage into smaller pieces using a spatula or spoon. Cook for 3 to 4 minutes, until the sausage is brown. 5. Add the salsa and scrambled eggs. Stir to combine. Remove the skillet from heat. 6. Spoon the mixture evenly onto the tortillas. 7. To form the burritos, fold the sides of each tortilla in toward the middle and then roll up from the bottom. You can secure each burrito with a toothpick. Or you can moisten the outside edge of the tortilla with a small amount of water. I prefer to use a cooking brush, but you can also dab with your fingers. 8. Spray the burritos with cooking oil and place them in the two air fryer drawers. Do not stack. Air fry at 204°C for 8 minutes. 9. Open the air fryer and flip the burritos. Cook for an additional 2 minutes or until crisp. 10. Sprinkle the Cheddar cheese over the burritos. Cool before serving.

Cajun Breakfast Sausage

Prep time: 10 minutes | Cook time: 15 to 20 minutes
| Serves 8

680 g 85% lean turkey mince
3 cloves garlic, finely chopped
¼ onion, grated
1 teaspoon Tabasco sauce

1 teaspoon Cajun seasoning
1 teaspoon dried thyme
½ teaspoon paprika
½ teaspoon cayenne

1. Preheat the air fryer to 188°C. 2. In a large bowl, combine the turkey, garlic, onion, Tabasco, Cajun seasoning, thyme, paprika, and cayenne. Mix with clean hands until thoroughly combined. Shape into 16 patties, about ½ inch thick. (Wet your hands slightly if you find the sausage too sticky to handle.) 3. Arrange the patties in a single layer in the two air fryer drawers. Pausing halfway through the cooking time to flip the patties, air fry for 15 to 20 minutes until a thermometer inserted into the thickest portion registers 74°C.

Bacon and Spinach Egg Muffins

Prep time: 7 minutes | Cook time: 12 to 14 minutes |
Serves 6

6 large eggs
60 ml double (whipping) cream
½ teaspoon sea salt
¼ teaspoon freshly ground
black pepper
¼ teaspoon cayenne pepper

(optional)
180 ml frozen chopped spinach,
thawed and drained
4 strips cooked bacon, crumbled
60 g shredded Cheddar cheese

1. In a large bowl (with a spout if you have one), whisk together the eggs, double cream, salt, black pepper, and cayenne pepper (if using). 2. Divide the spinach and bacon among 6 silicone muffin cups. Place the muffin cups in the zone 1 air fryer drawer. 3. Divide the egg mixture among the muffin cups. Top with the cheese. 4. Set the temperature to 150°C. Bake for 12 to 14 minutes, until the eggs are set and cooked through.

Breakfast Sausage and Cauliflower

Prep time: 5 minutes | Cook time: 45 minutes | Serves 4

450 g sausage meat, cooked and
crumbled
475 ml double/whipping cream
1 head cauliflower, chopped
235 ml grated Cheddar cheese,

plus more for topping
8 eggs, beaten
Salt and ground black pepper,
to taste

1. Preheat the air fryer to 176°C. 2. In a large bowl, mix the sausage, cream, chopped cauliflower, cheese and eggs. Sprinkle with salt and ground black pepper. 3. Pour the mixture into a greased casserole dish. Bake in the preheated air fryer for 45 minutes or until firm. 4. Top with more Cheddar cheese and serve.

Cinnamon Rolls

Prep time: 10 minutes | Cook time: 20 minutes | Makes 12 rolls

600 ml shredded Mozzarella cheese	½ teaspoon vanilla extract
60 g cream cheese, softened	120 ml icing sugar-style sweetener
235 ml blanched finely ground almond flour	1 tablespoon ground cinnamon

1. In a large microwave-safe bowl, combine Mozzarella cheese, cream cheese, and flour. Microwave the mixture on high 90 seconds until cheese is melted. 2. Add vanilla extract and sweetener, and mix 2 minutes until a dough forms. 3. Once the dough is cool enough to work with your hands, about 2 minutes, spread it out into a 12 × 4-inch rectangle on ungreased parchment paper. Evenly sprinkle dough with cinnamon. 4. Starting at the long side of the dough, roll lengthwise to form a log. Slice the log into twelve even pieces. 5. Divide rolls between two ungreased round nonstick baking dishes. Place the dishes into the two air fryer drawers. Adjust the temperature to 192ºC and bake for 10 minutes. 6. Cinnamon rolls will be done when golden around the edges and mostly firm. Allow rolls to cool in dishes 10 minutes before serving.

Whole Grain Eggs Avocado Toast and Butternut Squash and Ricotta Frittata

Prep time: 15 minutes | Cook time: 33 minutes | Serves 7

Whole Grain Eggs Avocado Toast:	Frittata:
Olive oil cooking spray	235 ml cubed (½-inch) butternut squash (160 g)
4 large eggs	2 tablespoons olive oil
Salt	Coarse or flaky salt and freshly ground black pepper, to taste
Black pepper	
4 pieces wholegrain bread	4 fresh sage leaves, thinly sliced
1 avocado	6 large eggs, lightly beaten
Red pepper flakes (optional)	120 ml ricotta cheese
Butternut Squash and Ricotta	Cayenne pepper

Make the Whole Grain Eggs Avocado Toast (zone 1 drawer): 1. Preheat the air fryer to 160ºC. Lightly coat the inside of four small oven-safe ramekins with olive oil cooking spray. 2. Crack one egg into each ramekin, and season with salt and black pepper. 3. Place the ramekins into the zone 1 air fryer drawer. Close and set the timer to 7 minutes. 4. While the eggs are cooking, toast the bread in a toaster. 5. Slice the avocado in half lengthwise, remove the pit, and scoop the flesh into a small bowl. Season with salt, black pepper, and red pepper flakes, if desired. Using a fork, smash the avocado lightly. 6. Spread a quarter of the smashed avocado evenly over each slice of toast. 7. Remove the eggs from the air fryer, and gently spoon one onto each slice of avocado toast before serving.
Make the Butternut Squash and Ricotta Frittata (zone 2 drawer):

1. In a bowl, toss the squash with the olive oil and season with salt and black pepper until evenly coated. Sprinkle the sage on the bottom of a cake pan and place the squash on top. Place the pan in the zone 2 air fryer drawer and bake at 204ºC for 10 minutes. Stir to incorporate the sage, then cook until the squash is tender and lightly caramelized at the edges, about 3 minutes more. 2. Pour the eggs over the squash, dollop the ricotta all over, and sprinkle with cayenne. Bake at 150ºC until the eggs are set and the frittata is golden brown on top, about 20 minutes. Remove the pan from the air fryer and cut the frittata into wedges to serve.

Parmesan Sausage Egg Muffins

Prep time: 5 minutes | Cook time: 20 minutes | Serves 4

170 g Italian-seasoned sausage, sliced	Salt and ground black pepper, to taste
6 eggs	85 g Parmesan cheese, grated
30 ml double cream	

1. Preheat the air fryer to 176ºC. Grease a muffin pan. 2. Put the sliced sausage in the muffin pan. 3. Beat the eggs with the cream in a bowl and season with salt and pepper. 4. Pour half of the mixture over the sausages in the pan. 5. Sprinkle with cheese and the remaining egg mixture. 6. Bake in the preheated air fryer for 20 minutes or until set. 7. Serve immediately.

sparagus and Bell Pepper Strata and Greek Wholemeal Banana-Walnut Bread

Prep time: 10 minutes | Cook time: 23 minutes | Serves 6

Olive oil cooking spray	2 tablespoons honey
2 ripe medium bananas	235 ml wholemeal flour
1 large egg	¼ teaspoon salt
60 ml non-fat plain Greek yoghurt	¼ teaspoon baking soda
60 ml olive oil	½ teaspoon ground cinnamon
½ teaspoon vanilla extract	60 ml chopped walnuts

1. Preheat the zone 1 air fryer drawer to 182ºC. Lightly coat the inside of a 8-by-4-inch loaf pan with olive oil cooking spray. (Or use two 5 ½-by-3-inch loaf pans.) 2. In a large bowl, mash the bananas with a fork. Add the egg, yoghurt, olive oil, vanilla, and honey. Mix until well combined and mostly smooth. 3. Sift the wholemeal flour, salt, baking soda, and cinnamon into the wet mixture, then stir until just combined. Do not overmix. 4. Gently fold in the walnuts. 5. Pour into the prepared loaf pan and spread to distribute evenly. 6. Place the loaf pan in the zone 1 air fryer drawer and bake for 20 to 23 minutes, or until golden brown on top and a toothpick inserted into the center comes out clean. 7. Allow to cool for 5 minutes before serving.

Gyro Breakfast Patties with Tzatziki

Prep time: 10 minutes | Cook time: 20 minutes | Makes 16

patties
Patties:
900 g lamb or beef mince
120 ml diced red onions
60 ml sliced black olives
2 tablespoons tomato sauce
1 teaspoon dried oregano leaves
2 cloves garlic, minced
1 teaspoon fine sea salt
Tzatziki:
235 ml full-fat sour cream
1 small cucumber, chopped

½ teaspoon fine sea salt
½ teaspoon garlic powder, or 1
clove garlic, minced
¼ teaspoon dried dill, or 1
teaspoon finely chopped fresh
dill
For Garnish/Serving:
120 ml crumbled feta cheese
(about 60 g)
Diced red onions
Sliced black olives
Sliced cucumbers

1. Preheat the air fryer to 176°C. 2. Place the lamb, onions, olives, tomato sauce, oregano, garlic, and salt in a large bowl. Mix well to combine the ingredients. 3. Using your hands, form the mixture into sixteen 3-inch patties. Place the patties in the two air fryer drawers and air fry for 20 minutes, flipping halfway through. Remove the patties and place them on a serving platter. 4. While the patties cook, make the tzatziki: Place all the ingredients in a small bowl and stir well. Cover and store in the fridge until ready to serve. Garnish with ground black pepper before serving. 5. Serve the patties with a dollop of tzatziki, a sprinkle of crumbled feta cheese, diced red onions, sliced black olives, and sliced cucumbers. 6. Store leftovers in an airtight container in the refrigerator for up to 5 days or in the freezer for up to a month. Reheat the patties in a preheated 200°C air fryer for a few minutes, until warmed through.

Cauliflower Avocado Toast and All-in-One Toast

Prep time: 25 minutes | Cook time: 10 minutes | Serves 3

Cauliflower Avocado Toast:
1 (40 g) steamer bag cauliflower
1 large egg
120 ml shredded Mozzarella
cheese
1 ripe medium avocado
½ teaspoon garlic powder
¼ teaspoon ground black
pepper

All-in-One Toast:
1 strip bacon, diced
1 slice 1-inch thick bread
1 egg
Salt and freshly ground black
pepper, to taste
60 ml grated Monterey Jack or
Chedday cheese

Make the Cauliflower Avocado Toast (zone 1 drawer): 1. Cook cauliflower according to package instructions. Remove from bag and place into cheesecloth or clean towel to remove excess moisture. 2. Place cauliflower into a large bowl and mix in egg and Mozzarella. Cut a piece of parchment to fit your air fryer drawer. Separate the cauliflower mixture into two, and place it on the parchment in two mounds. Press out the cauliflower mounds into a ¼-inch-thick rectangle. Place the parchment into the zone 1 air

fryer drawer. 3. Adjust the temperature to 204°C and set the timer for 8 minutes. 4. Flip the cauliflower halfway through the cooking time. 5. When the timer beeps, remove the parchment and allow the cauliflower to cool 5 minutes. 6. Cut open the avocado and remove the pit. Scoop out the inside, place it in a medium bowl, and mash it with garlic powder and pepper. Spread onto the cauliflower. Serve immediately.

Make the All-in-One Toast (zone 2 drawer): 1. Preheat the zone 2 air fryer drawer to 204°C. 2. Air fry the bacon for 3 minutes, shaking the zone 2 drawer once or twice while it cooks. Remove the bacon to a paper towel lined plate and set aside. 3. Use a sharp paring knife to score a large circle in the middle of the slice of bread, cutting halfway through, but not all the way through to the cutting board. Press down on the circle in the center of the bread slice to create an indentation. 4. Transfer the slice of bread, hole side up, to the air fryer drawer. Crack the egg into the center of the bread, and season with salt and pepper. 5. Adjust the air fryer temperature to 192°C and air fry for 5 minutes. Sprinkle the grated cheese around the edges of the bread, leaving the center of the yolk uncovered, and top with the cooked bacon. Press the cheese and bacon into the bread lightly to help anchor it to the bread and prevent it from blowing around in the air fryer. 6. Air fry for one or two more minutes, just to melt the cheese and finish cooking the egg. Serve immediately.

AMozzarella Bacon Calzones

Prep time: 15 minutes | Cook time: 12 minutes | Serves 4

2 large eggs
235 ml blanched finely ground
almond flour
475 ml shredded Mozzarella
cheese

60 g cream cheese, softened
and broken into small pieces
4 slices cooked bacon,
crumbled

1. Beat eggs in a small bowl. Pour into a medium nonstick skillet over medium heat and scramble. Set aside. 2. In a large microwave-safe bowl, mix flour and Mozzarella. Add cream cheese to the bowl. 3. Place bowl in microwave and cook 45 seconds on high to melt cheese, then stir with a fork until a soft dough ball forms. 4. Cut a piece of parchment to fit air fryer drawer. Separate dough into two sections and press each out into an 8-inch round. 5. On half of each dough round, place half of the scrambled eggs and crumbled bacon. Fold the other side of the dough over and press to seal the edges. 6. Place calzones on ungreased parchment and into the zone 1 air fryer drawer. Adjust the temperature to 176°C and set the timer for 12 minutes, turning calzones halfway through cooking. Crust will be golden and firm when done. 7. Let calzones cool on a cooking rack 5 minutes before serving.

Onion Omelette and Buffalo Egg Cups

Prep time: 20 minutes | Cook time: 15 minutes | Serves 4

Onion Omelette:	Cooking spray
3 eggs	Buffalo Egg Cups:
Salt and ground black pepper,	4 large eggs
to taste	60 g full-fat cream cheese
½ teaspoons soy sauce	2 tablespoons buffalo sauce
1 large onion, chopped	120 ml shredded sharp Cheddar
2 tablespoons grated Cheddar	cheese
cheese	

Make the Onion Omelette (zone 1 drawer): 1. Preheat the zone 1 air fryer drawer to 180ºC. 2. In a bowl, whisk together the eggs, salt, pepper, and soy sauce. 3. Spritz a small pan with cooking spray. Spread the chopped onion across the bottom of the pan, then transfer the pan to the zone 1 air fryer drawer. 4. Bake in the preheated air fryer for 6 minutes or until the onion is translucent. 5. Add the egg mixture on top of the onions to coat well. Add the cheese on top, then continue baking for another 6 minutes. 6. Allow to cool before serving.

Make the Buffalo Egg Cups (zone 2 drawer): 1. Crack eggs into two ramekins. 2. In a small microwave-safe bowl, mix cream cheese, buffalo sauce, and Cheddar. Microwave for 20 seconds and then stir. Place a spoonful into each ramekin on top of the eggs. 3. Place ramekins into the zone 2 air fryer drawer. 4. Adjust the temperature to 160ºC and bake for 15 minutes. 5. Serve warm.

Bacon Cheese Egg with Avocado and Potato Nuggets

Prep time: 25 minutes | Cook time: 20 minutes | Serves 8

Bacon Cheese Egg with	12 slices bacon, cooked and
Avocado:	crumbled
6 large eggs	Potato Nuggets:
60 ml double cream	1 teaspoon extra virgin olive oil
350 ml chopped cauliflower	1 clove garlic, minced
235 ml shredded medium	1 L kale, rinsed and chopped
Cheddar cheese	475 ml potatoes, boiled and
1 medium avocado, peeled and	mashed
pitted	30 ml milk
8 tablespoons full-fat sour	Salt and ground black pepper,
cream	to taste
2 spring onions, sliced on the	Cooking spray
bias	

Make the Bacon Cheese Egg with Avocado (zone 1 drawer): 1. In a medium bowl, whisk eggs and cream together. Pour into a round baking dish. 2. Add cauliflower and mix, then top with Cheddar. Place dish into the zone 1 air fryer drawer. 3. Adjust the temperature to 160ºC and set the timer for 20 minutes. 4. When completely cooked, eggs will be firm and cheese will be browned. Slice into four pieces. 5. Slice avocado and divide evenly among pieces. Top each piece with 2 tablespoons sour cream, sliced spring onions, and crumbled bacon.

Make the Potato Nuggets (zone 2 drawer): 1. Preheat the zone 2 air fryer drawer to 200ºC. 2. In a skillet over medium heat, sauté the garlic in the olive oil, until it turns golden brown. Sauté with the kale for an additional 3 minutes and remove from the heat. 3. Mix the mashed potatoes, kale and garlic in a bowl. Pour in the milk and sprinkle with salt and pepper. 4. Shape the mixture into nuggets and spritz with cooking spray. 5. Put in the zone 2 air fryer drawer and air fry for 15 minutes, flip the nuggets halfway through cooking to make sure the nuggets fry evenly. 6. Serve immediately.

Bacon, Cheese, and Avocado Melt & Cheesy Scrambled Eggs

Prep time: 7 minutes | Cook time: 9 minutes | Serves 4

Bacon, Cheese, and Avocado	1 teaspoon unsalted butter
Melt:	2 large eggs
1 avocado	2 tablespoons milk
4 slices cooked bacon, chopped	2 tablespoons shredded Cheddar
2 tablespoons salsa	cheese
1 tablespoon double cream	Salt and freshly ground black
60 ml shredded Cheddar cheese	pepper, to taste
Cheesy Scrambled Eggs:	

Make the Bacon, Cheese, and Avocado Melt (zone 1 drawer): 1. Preheat the zone 1 air fryer drawer to 204ºC. 2. Slice the avocado in half lengthwise and remove the stone. To ensure the avocado halves do not roll in the drawer, slice a thin piece of skin off the base. 3. In a small bowl, combine the bacon, salsa, and cream. Divide the mixture between the avocado halves and top with the cheese. 4. Place the avocado halves in the zone 1 air fryer drawer and air fry for 3 to 5 minutes until the cheese has melted and begins to brown. Serve warm.

Make the Cheesy Scrambled Eggs (zone 2 drawer): 1. Preheat the zone 2 air fryer drawer to 150ºC. Place the butter in a baking pan and cook for 1 to 2 minutes, until melted. 2. In a small bowl, whisk together the eggs, milk, and cheese. Season with salt and black pepper. Transfer the mixture to the pan. 3. Cook for 3 minutes. Stir the eggs and push them toward the center of the pan. 4. Cook for another 2 minutes, then stir again. Cook for another 2 minutes, until the eggs are just cooked. Serve warm.

Wholemeal Blueberry Muffins

Prep time: 10 minutes | Cook time: 15 minutes | Serves 6

Olive oil cooking spray
120 ml unsweetened applesauce
60 ml honey
120 ml non-fat plain Greek yoghurt
1 teaspoon vanilla extract
1 large egg

350 ml plus 1 tablespoon wholemeal, divided
½ teaspoon baking soda
½ teaspoon baking powder
½ teaspoon salt
120 ml blueberries, fresh or frozen

1. Preheat the zone 1 air fryer drawer to 182°C. Lightly coat the inside of six silicone muffin cups or a six-cup muffin tin with olive oil cooking spray. 2. In a large bowl, combine the applesauce, honey, yoghurt, vanilla, and egg and mix until smooth. 3. Sift in 350 ml of the flour, the baking soda, baking powder, and salt into the wet mixture, then stir until just combined. 4. In a small bowl, toss the blueberries with the remaining 1 tablespoon flour, then fold the mixture into the muffin batter. 5. Divide the mixture evenly among the prepared muffin cups and place into the zone 1 drawer of the air fryer. Bake for 12 to 15 minutes, or until golden brown on top and a toothpick inserted into the middle of one of the muffins comes out clean. 6. Allow to cool for 5 minutes before serving.

Chapter 3 Poultry

Chapter 3 Poultry

Pecan-Crusted Chicken Tenders

Prep time: 10 minutes | Cook time: 12 minutes | Serves 4

2 tablespoons mayonnaise	¼ teaspoon ground black
1 teaspoon Dijon mustard	pepper
455 g boneless, skinless chicken	75 g chopped roasted pecans,
tenders	finely ground
½ teaspoon salt	

1. In a small bowl, whisk mayonnaise and mustard until combined. Brush mixture onto chicken tenders on both sides, then sprinkle tenders with salt and pepper. 2. Place pecans in a medium bowl and press each tender into pecans to coat each side. 3. Place tenders into the two ungreased air fryer drawers in a single layer. Adjust the temperature to 190°C and roast for 12 minutes, turning tenders halfway through cooking. Tenders will be golden brown and have an internal temperature of at least 76°C when done. Serve warm.

Garlic Dill Wings

Prep time: 5 minutes | Cook time: 25 minutes | Serves 4

900 g bone-in chicken wings,	pepper
separated at joints	½ teaspoon onion powder
½ teaspoon salt	½ teaspoon garlic powder
½ teaspoon ground black	1 teaspoon dried dill

1. In a large bowl, toss wings with salt, pepper, onion powder, garlic powder, and dill until evenly coated. Place wings into the two ungreased air fryer drawers in a single layer. 2. Adjust the temperature to 200°C and air fry for 25 minutes, shaking the drawer every 7 minutes during cooking. Wings should have an internal temperature of at least 76°C and be golden brown when done. Serve warm.

Crispy Dill Chicken Strips

Prep time: 30 minutes | Cook time: 10 minutes | Serves 4

2 whole boneless, skinless	1 tablespoon dried dill weed
chicken breasts (about 450 g	1 tablespoon garlic powder
each), halved lengthwise	1 large egg, beaten
230 ml Italian dressing	1 to 2 tablespoons oil
110 g finely crushed crisps	

1. In a large resealable bag, combine the chicken and Italian dressing. Seal the bag and refrigerate to marinate at least 1 hour. 2. In a shallow dish, stir together the potato chips, dill, and garlic powder. Place the beaten egg in a second shallow dish. 3. Remove the chicken from the marinade. Roll the chicken pieces in the egg and the crisp mixture, coating thoroughly. 4. Preheat the air fryer to 170°C. Line the two air fryer drawers with parchment paper. 5. Place the coated chicken on the parchment and spritz with oil. 6. Cook for 5 minutes. Flip the chicken, spritz it with oil, and cook for 5 minutes more until the outsides are crispy and the insides are no longer pink.

Cracked-Pepper Chicken Wings

Prep time: 15 minutes | Cook time: 20 minutes | Serves 4

450 g chicken wings	½ teaspoon garlic powder
3 tablespoons vegetable oil	½ teaspoon kosher salt
60 g all-purpose flour	1½ teaspoons freshly cracked
½ teaspoon smoked paprika	black pepper

1. Place the chicken wings in a large bowl. Drizzle the vegetable oil over wings and toss to coat. 2. In a separate bowl, whisk together the flour, paprika, garlic powder, salt, and pepper until combined. 3. Dredge the wings in the flour mixture one at a time, coating them well, and place in the zone 1 air fryer drawer. Set the temperature to 200°C for 20 minutes, turning the wings halfway through the cooking time, until the breading is browned and crunchy.

Coriander Lime Chicken Thighs

Prep time: 15 minutes | Cook time: 22 minutes | Serves 4

4 bone-in, skin-on chicken	2 teaspoons chili powder
thighs	1 teaspoon cumin
1 teaspoon baking powder	2 medium limes
½ teaspoon garlic powder	5 g chopped fresh coriander

1. Pat chicken thighs dry and sprinkle with baking powder. 2. In a small bowl, mix garlic powder, chili powder, and cumin and sprinkle evenly over thighs, gently rubbing on and under chicken skin. 3. Cut one lime in half and squeeze juice over thighs. Place chicken into the zone 1 air fryer drawer. 4. Adjust the temperature to 190°C and roast for 22 minutes. 5. Cut other lime into four wedges for serving and garnish cooked chicken with wedges and coriander.

Curried Orange Honey Chicken

Prep time: 10 minutes | Cook time: 16 to 19 minutes | Serves 4

340 g boneless, skinless chicken thighs, cut into 1-inch pieces	60 ml chicken stock
1 yellow bell pepper, cut into 1½-inch pieces	2 tablespoons honey
1 small red onion, sliced	60 ml orange juice
Olive oil for misting	1 tablespoon cornflour
	2 to 3 teaspoons curry powder

1. Preheat the air fryer to 190ºC. 2. Put the chicken thighs, pepper, and red onion in the zone 1 air fryer drawer and mist with olive oil. 3. Roast for 12 to 14 minutes or until the chicken is cooked to 76ºC, shaking the drawer halfway through cooking time. 4. Remove the chicken and vegetables from the air fryer drawer and set aside. 5. In a metal bowl, combine the stock, honey, orange juice, cornflour, and curry powder, and mix well. Add the chicken and vegetables, stir, and put the bowl in the drawer. 6. Return the drawer to the air fryer and roast for 2 minutes. Remove and stir, then roast for 2 to 3 minutes or until the sauce is thickened and bubbly. 7. Serve warm.

Thai Curry Meatballs

Prep time: 10 minutes | Cook time: 10 minutes | Serves 4

450 g chicken mince	1 tablespoon fish sauce
15 g chopped fresh coriander	2 garlic cloves, minced
1 teaspoon chopped fresh mint	2 teaspoons minced fresh ginger
1 tablespoon fresh lime juice	½ teaspoon kosher salt
1 tablespoon Thai red, green, or yellow curry paste	½ teaspoon black pepper
	¼ teaspoon red pepper flakes

1. Preheat the zone 1 air fryer drawer to 200ºC. 2. In a large bowl, gently mix the chicken mince, coriander, mint, lime juice, curry paste, fish sauce, garlic, ginger, salt, black pepper, and red pepper flakes until thoroughly combined. 3. Form the mixture into 16 meatballs. Place the meatballs in a single layer in the zone 1 air fryer drawer. Air fry for 10 minutes, turning the meatballs halfway through the cooking time. Use a meat thermometer to ensure the meatballs have reached an internal temperature of 76ºC. Serve immediately.

Apricot-Glazed Turkey Tenderloin

Prep time: 20 minutes | Cook time: 30 minutes | Serves 4

Olive oil	mustard
80 g sugar-free apricot preserves	680 g turkey breast tenderloin
½ tablespoon spicy brown	Salt and freshly ground black pepper, to taste

1. Spray the two air fryer drawers lightly with olive oil. 2. In a small bowl, combine the apricot preserves and mustard to make a paste. 3. Season the turkey with salt and pepper. Spread the apricot paste all over the turkey. 4. Place the turkey in the two air fryer drawers and lightly spray with olive oil. 5. Air fry at 190ºC for 15 minutes. Flip the turkey over and lightly spray with olive oil. Air fry until the internal temperature reaches at least 80ºC, an additional 10 to 15 minutes. 6. Let the turkey rest for 10 minutes before slicing and serving.

Nice Goulash

Prep time: 5 minutes | Cook time: 17 minutes | Serves 2

2 red bell peppers, chopped	Salt and ground black pepper, to taste
450 g chicken mince	Cooking spray
2 medium tomatoes, diced	
120 ml chicken broth	

1. Preheat the zone 1 air fryer drawer to 186ºC. Spritz a baking pan with cooking spray. 2. Set the bell pepper in the baking pan and put in the zone 1 air fry drawer to broil for 5 minutes or until the bell pepper is tender. Shake the drawer halfway through. 3. Add the chicken mince and diced tomatoes in the baking pan and stir to mix well. Broil for 6 more minutes or until the chicken is lightly browned. 4. Pour the chicken broth over and sprinkle with salt and ground black pepper. Stir to mix well. Broil for an additional 6 minutes. 5. Serve immediately.

Hawaiian Chicken Bites

Prep time: 1 hour 15 minutes | Cook time: 15 minutes | Serves 4

120 ml pineapple juice	110 g brown sugar
2 tablespoons apple cider vinegar	2 tablespoons sherry
½ tablespoon minced ginger	120 ml soy sauce
120 g ketchup	4 chicken breasts, cubed
2 garlic cloves, minced	Cooking spray

1. Combine the pineapple juice, cider vinegar, ginger, ketchup, garlic, and sugar in a saucepan. Stir to mix well. Heat over low heat for 5 minutes or until thickened. Fold in the sherry and soy sauce. 2. Dunk the chicken cubes in the mixture. Press to submerge. Wrap the bowl in plastic and refrigerate to marinate for at least an hour. 3. Preheat the air fryer to 180ºC. Spritz the two air fryer drawers with cooking spray. 4. Remove the chicken cubes from the marinade. Shake the excess off and put in the preheated air fryer. Spritz with cooking spray. 5. Air fry for 15 minutes or until the chicken cubes are glazed and well browned. Shake the drawer at least three times during the frying. 6. Serve immediately.

Chicken Legs with Leeks

Prep time: 30 minutes | Cook time: 18 minutes | Serves 6

2 leeks, sliced
2 large-sized tomatoes, chopped
3 cloves garlic, minced
½ teaspoon dried oregano
6 chicken legs, boneless and

skinless
½ teaspoon smoked cayenne pepper
2 tablespoons olive oil
A freshly ground nutmeg

1. In a mixing dish, thoroughly combine all ingredients, minus the leeks. Place in the refrigerator and let it marinate overnight. 2. Lay the leeks onto the bottom of the two air fryer drawers. Top with the chicken legs. 3. Roast chicken legs at 190ºC for 18 minutes, turning halfway through. Serve with hoisin sauce.

Honey-Glazed Chicken Thighs

Prep time: 5 minutes | Cook time: 14 minutes | Serves 4

Oil, for spraying
4 boneless, skinless chicken thighs, fat trimmed
3 tablespoons soy sauce

1 tablespoon balsamic vinegar
2 teaspoons honey
2 teaspoons minced garlic
1 teaspoon ground ginger

1. Preheat the zone 1 air fryer drawer to 200ºC. Line the zone 1 air fryer drawer with parchment and spray lightly with oil. 2. Place the chicken in the prepared drawer. 3. Cook for 7 minutes, flip, and cook for another 7 minutes, or until the internal temperature reaches 76ºC and the juices run clear. 4. In a small saucepan, combine the soy sauce, balsamic vinegar, honey, garlic, and ginger and cook over low heat for 1 to 2 minutes, until warmed through. 5. Transfer the chicken to a serving plate and drizzle with the sauce just before serving.

Indian Fennel Chicken

Prep time: 30 minutes | Cook time: 15 minutes | Serves 4

450 g boneless, skinless chicken thighs, cut crosswise into thirds
1 yellow onion, cut into 1½-inch-thick slices
1 tablespoon coconut oil, melted
2 teaspoons minced fresh ginger
2 teaspoons minced garlic
1 teaspoon smoked paprika

1 teaspoon ground fennel
1 teaspoon garam masala
1 teaspoon ground turmeric
1 teaspoon kosher salt
½ to 1 teaspoon cayenne pepper
Vegetable oil spray
2 teaspoons fresh lemon juice
5 g chopped fresh coriander or parsley

1. Use a fork to pierce the chicken all over to allow the marinade to penetrate better. 2. In a large bowl, combine the onion, coconut oil, ginger, garlic, paprika, fennel, garam masala, turmeric, salt, and cayenne. Add the chicken, toss to combine, and marinate at room temperature for 30 minutes, or cover and refrigerate for up to 24 hours. 3. Place the chicken and onion in the zone 1 air fryer drawer. (Discard remaining marinade.) Spray with some vegetable

oil spray. Set the air fryer to 180ºC for 15 minutes. Halfway through the cooking time, remove the drawer, spray the chicken and onion with more vegetable oil spray, and toss gently to coat. At the end of the cooking time, use a meat thermometer to ensure the chicken has reached an internal temperature of 76ºC. 4. Transfer the chicken and onion to a serving platter. Sprinkle with the lemon juice and coriander and serve.

Broccoli and Cheese Stuffed Chicken

Prep time: 15 minutes | Cook time: 20 minutes | Serves 4

60 g cream cheese, softened
70 g chopped fresh broccoli, steamed
120 g shredded sharp Cheddar cheese
4 (170 g) boneless, skinless

chicken breasts
2 tablespoons mayonnaise
¼ teaspoon salt
¼ teaspoon garlic powder
⅛ teaspoon ground black pepper

1. In a medium bowl, combine cream cheese, broccoli, and Cheddar. Cut a 4-inch pocket into each chicken breast. Evenly divide mixture between chicken breasts; stuff the pocket of each chicken breast with the mixture. 2. Spread ¼ tablespoon mayonnaise per side of each chicken breast, then sprinkle both sides of breasts with salt, garlic powder, and pepper. 3. Place stuffed chicken breasts into the two ungreased air fryer drawers so that the open seams face up. Adjust the temperature to 180ºC and air fry for 20 minutes, turning chicken halfway through cooking. When done, chicken will be golden and have an internal temperature of at least 76ºC. Serve warm.

Jerk Chicken Thighs

Prep time: 30 minutes | Cook time: 15 to 20 minutes | Serves 6

2 teaspoons ground coriander
1 teaspoon ground allspice
1 teaspoon cayenne pepper
1 teaspoon ground ginger
1 teaspoon salt
1 teaspoon dried thyme

½ teaspoon ground cinnamon
½ teaspoon ground nutmeg
900 g boneless chicken thighs, skin on
2 tablespoons olive oil

1. In a small bowl, combine the coriander, allspice, cayenne, ginger, salt, thyme, cinnamon, and nutmeg. Stir until thoroughly combined. 2. Place the chicken in a baking dish and use paper towels to pat dry. Thoroughly coat both sides of the chicken with the spice mixture. Cover and refrigerate for at least 2 hours, preferably overnight. 3. Preheat the air fryer to 180ºC. 4. Arrange the chicken in a single layer in the two air fryer drawers and lightly coat with the olive oil. Pausing halfway through the cooking time to flip the chicken, air fry for 15 to 20 minutes, until a thermometer inserted into the thickest part registers 76ºC.

Greek Chicken Souvlaki

Prep time: 30 minutes | Cook time: 15 minutes | Serves 3 to 4

Chicken:
Grated zest and juice of 1 lemon
2 tablespoons extra-virgin olive oil
1 tablespoon Greek souvlaki seasoning
450 g boneless, skinless chicken breast, cut into 2-inch chunks

Vegetable oil spray
For Serving:
Warm pita bread or hot cooked rice
Sliced ripe tomatoes
Sliced cucumbers
Thinly sliced red onion
Kalamata olives
Tzatziki

1. For the chicken: In a small bowl, combine the lemon zest, lemon juice, olive oil, and souvlaki seasoning. Place the chicken in a gallon-size resealable plastic bag. Pour the marinade over chicken. Seal bag and massage to coat. Place the bag in a large bowl and marinate for 30 minutes, or cover and refrigerate up to 24 hours, turning the bag occasionally. 2. Place the chicken a single layer in the zone 1 air fryer drawer. Cook at 180°C for 10 minutes, turning the chicken and spraying with a little vegetable oil spray halfway through the cooking time. Increase the air fryer temperature to 200°C for 5 minutes to allow the chicken to crisp and brown a little. 3. Transfer the chicken to a serving platter and serve with pita bread or rice, tomatoes, cucumbers, onion, olives and tzatziki.

Chicken Patties and One-Dish Chicken Rice

Prep time: 25 minutes | Cook time: 40 minutes | Serves 8

Chicken Patties:
450 g chicken thigh mince
110 g shredded Mozzarella cheese
1 teaspoon dried parsley
½ teaspoon garlic powder
¼ teaspoon onion powder
1 large egg
60 g pork rinds, finely ground
One-Dish Chicken and Rice:
190 g long-grain white rice,

rinsed and drained
120 g cut frozen green beans (do not thaw)
1 tablespoon minced fresh ginger
3 cloves garlic, minced
1 tablespoon toasted sesame oil
1 teaspoon kosher salt
1 teaspoon black pepper
450 g chicken wings, preferably drumettes

Make the Chicken Patties (zone 1 drawer): 1. In a large bowl, mix chicken mince, Mozzarella, parsley, garlic powder, and onion powder. Form into four patties. 2. Place patties in the freezer for 15 to 20 minutes until they begin to firm up. 3. Whisk egg in a medium bowl. Place the ground pork rinds into a large bowl. 4. Dip each chicken patty into the egg and then press into pork rinds to fully coat. Place patties into the zone 1 air fryer drawer. 5. Adjust the temperature to 180°C and air fry for 12 minutes. 6. Patties will be firm and cooked to an internal temperature of 76°C when done. Serve immediately.
Make the One-Dish Chicken and Rice (zone 2 drawer): 1. In a baking pan, combine the rice, green beans, ginger, garlic, sesame

oil, salt, and pepper. Stir to combine. Place the chicken wings on top of the rice mixture. 2. Cover the pan with foil. Make a long slash in the foil to allow the pan to vent steam. Place the pan in the zone 2 air fryer drawer. Set the air fryer to 190°C for 30 minutes. 3. Remove the foil. Set the air fryer to 200°C for 10 minutes, or until the wings have browned and rendered fat into the rice and vegetables, turning the wings halfway through the cooking time.

Lemon Thyme Roasted Chicken

Prep time: 10 minutes | Cook time: 60 minutes | Serves 6

2 tablespoons baking powder
1 teaspoon smoked paprika
Sea salt and freshly ground black pepper, to taste
900 g chicken wings or chicken drumettes
Avocado oil spray

80 ml avocado oil
120 ml Buffalo hot sauce, such as Frank's RedHot
4 tablespoons unsalted butter
2 tablespoons apple cider vinegar
1 teaspoon minced garlic

1. In a large bowl, stir together the baking powder, smoked paprika, and salt and pepper to taste. Add the chicken wings and toss to coat. 2. Set the air fryer to 200°C. Spray the wings with oil. 3. Place the wings in the two drawers in a single layer and air fry for 20 to 25 minutes. Check with an instant-read thermometer and remove when they reach 70°C. Let rest until they reach 76°C. 4. While the wings are cooking, whisk together the avocado oil, hot sauce, butter, vinegar, and garlic in a small saucepan over medium-low heat until warm. 5. When the wings are done cooking, toss them with the Buffalo sauce. Serve warm.

Simply Terrific Turkey Meatballs

Prep time: 10 minutes | Cook time: 7 to 10 minutes | Serves 4

1 red bell pepper, seeded and coarsely chopped
2 cloves garlic, coarsely chopped
15 g chopped fresh parsley
680 g 85% lean turkey mince

1 egg, lightly beaten
45 g grated Parmesan cheese
1 teaspoon salt
½ teaspoon freshly ground black pepper

1. Preheat the air fryer to 200°C. 2. In a food processor fitted with a metal blade, combine the bell pepper, garlic, and parsley. Pulse until finely chopped. Transfer the vegetables to a large mixing bowl. 3. Add the turkey, egg, Parmesan, salt, and black pepper. Mix gently until thoroughly combined. Shape the mixture into 1¼-inch meatballs. 4. Arrange the meatballs in a single layer in the two air fryer drawers; coat lightly with olive oil spray. Pausing halfway through the cooking time to shake the drawer, air fry for 7 to 10 minutes, until lightly browned and a thermometer inserted into the centre of a meatball registers 76°C.

Broccoli Cheese Chicken

Prep time: 15 minutes | Cook time: 25 minutes | Serves 4

1 tablespoon avocado oil	additional for seasoning,
15 g chopped onion	divided
35 g finely chopped broccoli	¼ freshly ground black pepper,
115 g cream cheese, at room	plus additional for seasoning,
temperature	divided
60 g Cheddar cheese, shredded	900 g boneless, skinless chicken
1 teaspoon garlic powder	breasts
½ teaspoon sea salt, plus	1 teaspoon smoked paprika

1. Heat a medium skillet over medium-high heat and pour in the avocado oil. Add the onion and broccoli and cook, stirring occasionally, for 5 to 8 minutes, until the onion is tender. 2. Transfer to a large bowl and stir in the cream cheese, Cheddar cheese, and garlic powder, and season to taste with salt and pepper. 3. Hold a sharp knife parallel to the chicken breast and cut a long pocket into one side. Stuff the chicken pockets with the broccoli mixture, using toothpicks to secure the pockets around the filling. 4. In a small dish, combine the paprika, ½ teaspoon salt, and ¼ teaspoon pepper. Sprinkle this over the outside of the chicken. 5. Set the air fryer to 200ºC. Place the chicken in a single layer in the two air fryer drawers and cook for 14 to 16 minutes, until an instant-read thermometer reads 70ºC. Place the chicken on a plate and tent a piece of aluminum foil over the chicken. Allow to rest for 5 to 10 minutes before serving.

Chicken Strips with Satay Sauce

Prep time: 15 minutes | Cook time: 10 minutes | Serves 4

4 (170 g) boneless, skinless	fresh ginger
chicken breasts, sliced into 16	½ teaspoon hot sauce
(1-inch) strips	⅛ teaspoon stevia glycerite, or
1 teaspoon fine sea salt	2 to 3 drops liquid stevia
1 teaspoon paprika	For Garnish/Serving (Optional):
Sauce:	15 g chopped coriander leaves
60 g creamy almond butter (or	Red pepper flakes
sunflower seed butter for nut-	Sea salt flakes
free)	Thinly sliced red, orange, and
2 tablespoons chicken broth	yellow bell peppers
1½ tablespoons coconut vinegar	Special Equipment:
or unseasoned rice vinegar	16 wooden or bamboo skewers,
1 clove garlic, minced	soaked in water for 15 minutes
1 teaspoon peeled and minced	

1. Spray the zone 1 air fryer drawer with avocado oil. Preheat the air fryer to 200ºC. 2. Thread the chicken strips onto the skewers. Season on all sides with the salt and paprika. Place the chicken skewers in the air fryer drawer and air fry for 5 minutes, flip, and cook for another 5 minutes, until the chicken is cooked through and the internal temperature reaches 76ºC. 3. While the chicken skewers cook, make the sauce: In a medium-sized bowl, stir together all the sauce ingredients until well combined. Taste and adjust the sweetness and heat to your liking. 4. Garnish the chicken with coriander, red pepper flakes, and salt flakes, if desired, and serve with sliced bell peppers, if desired. Serve the sauce on the side. 5. Store leftovers in an airtight container in the fridge for up to 4 days or in the freezer for up to a month. Reheat in a preheated 180ºC air fryer for 3 minutes per side, or until heated through.

Air Fried Chicken Potatoes with Sun-Dried Tomato

Prep time: 15 minutes | Cook time: 25 minutes | Serves 2

2 teaspoons minced fresh	15 g oil-packed sun-dried
oregano, divided	tomatoes, patted dry and
2 teaspoons minced fresh	chopped
thyme, divided	1½ tablespoons red wine
2 teaspoons extra-virgin olive	vinegar
oil, plus extra as needed	1 tablespoon capers, rinsed and
450 g fingerling potatoes,	minced
unpeeled	1 small shallot, minced
2 (340 g) bone-in split chicken	Salt and ground black pepper,
breasts, trimmed	to taste
1 garlic clove, minced	

1. Preheat the zone 1 air fryer drawer to 180ºC. 2. Combine 1 teaspoon of oregano, 1 teaspoon of thyme, ¼ teaspoon of salt, ¼ teaspoon of ground black pepper, 1 teaspoons of olive oil in a large bowl. Add the potatoes and toss to coat well. 3. Combine the chicken with remaining thyme, oregano, and olive oil. Sprinkle with garlic, salt, and pepper. Toss to coat well. 4. Place the potatoes in the preheated air fryer drawer, then arrange the chicken on top of the potatoes. 5. Air fry for 25 minutes or until the internal temperature of the chicken reaches at least 76ºC and the potatoes are wilted. Flip the chicken and potatoes halfway through. 6. Meanwhile, combine the sun-dried tomatoes, vinegar, capers, and shallot in a separate large bowl. Sprinkle with salt and ground black pepper. Toss to mix well. 7. Remove the chicken and potatoes from the air fryer and allow to cool for 10 minutes. Serve with the sun-dried tomato mix.

Easy Cajun Chicken Drumsticks

Prep time: 5 minutes | Cook time: 40 minutes | Serves 5

1 tablespoon olive oil	seasoning
10 chicken drumsticks	Salt and ground black pepper,
1½ tablespoons Cajun	to taste

1. Preheat the air fryer to 200ºC. Grease the two air fryer drawers with olive oil. 2. On a clean work surface, rub the chicken drumsticks with Cajun seasoning, salt, and ground black pepper. 3. Arrange the seasoned chicken drumsticks in a single layer in the air fryer. 4. Air fry for 18 minutes or until lightly browned. Flip the drumsticks halfway through. 5. Remove the chicken drumsticks from the air fryer. Serve immediately.

Chicken Parmesan

Prep time: 15 minutes | Cook time: 10 minutes | Serves 4

Oil, for spraying
2 (230 g) boneless, skinless chicken breasts
120 g Italian-style bread crumbs
20 g grated Parmesan cheese,
plus 45 g shredded
4 tablespoons unsalted butter, melted
115 g marinara sauce

1. Preheat the air fryer to 180°C. Line the two air fryer drawers with parchment and spray lightly with oil. 2. Cut each chicken breast in half through its thickness to make 4 thin cutlets. Using a meat tenderizer, pound each cutlet until it is about ¾ inch thick. 3. On a plate, mix together the bread crumbs and grated Parmesan cheese. 4. Lightly brush the chicken with the melted butter, then dip into the bread crumb mixture. 5. Place the chicken in the two prepared drawers and spray lightly with oil. 6. Cook for 6 minutes. Top the chicken with the marinara and shredded Parmesan cheese, dividing evenly. Cook for another 3 to 4 minutes, or until golden brown, crispy, and the internal temperature reaches 76°C.

Chicken with Bacon and Tomato

Prep time: 25 minutes | Cook time: 10 minutes | Serves 4

4 medium-sized skin-on chicken drumsticks
1½ teaspoons herbs de Provence
Salt and pepper, to taste
1 tablespoon rice vinegar
2 tablespoons olive oil
2 garlic cloves, crushed
340 g crushed canned tomatoes
1 small-size leek, thinly sliced
2 slices smoked bacon, chopped

1. Sprinkle the chicken drumsticks with herbs de Provence, salt and pepper; then, drizzle them with rice vinegar and olive oil. 2. Cook in the baking pan at 180°C for 8 to 10 minutes. Pause the air fryer; stir in the remaining ingredients and continue to cook for 15 minutes longer; make sure to check them periodically. Bon appétit!

Herbed Turkey Breast with Simple Dijon Sauce

Prep time: 5 minutes | Cook time: 30 minutes | Serves 4

1 teaspoon chopped fresh sage
1 teaspoon chopped fresh tarragon
1 teaspoon chopped fresh thyme leaves
1 teaspoon chopped fresh rosemary leaves
1½ teaspoons sea salt
1 teaspoon ground black pepper
1 (900 g) turkey breast
3 tablespoons Dijon mustard
3 tablespoons butter, melted
Cooking spray

1. Preheat the air fryer to 200°C. Spritz the two air fryer drawers with cooking spray. 2. Combine the herbs, salt, and black pepper in a small bowl. Stir to mix well. Set aside. 3. Combine the Dijon mustard and butter in a separate bowl. Stir to mix well. 4. Rub the turkey with the herb mixture on a clean work surface, then brush the turkey with Dijon mixture. 5. Arrange the turkey in the two preheated air fryer drawers. Air fry for 30 minutes or until an instant-read thermometer inserted in the thickest part of the turkey breast reaches at least 76°C. 6. Transfer the cooked turkey breast on a large plate and slice to serve.

Juicy Paprika Chicken Breast

Prep time: 5 minutes | Cook time: 30 minutes | Serves 4

Oil, for spraying
4 (170 g) boneless, skinless chicken breasts
1 tablespoon olive oil
1 tablespoon paprika
1 tablespoon packed light brown sugar
½ teaspoon cayenne pepper
½ teaspoon onion powder
½ teaspoon granulated garlic

1. Line the two air fryer drawers with parchment and spray lightly with oil. 2. Brush the chicken with the olive oil. 3. In a small bowl, mix together the paprika, brown sugar, cayenne pepper, onion powder, and garlic and sprinkle it over the chicken. 4. Place the chicken in the two prepared drawers. 5. Air fry at 180°C for 15 minutes, flip, and cook for another 15 minutes, or until the internal temperature reaches 76°C. Serve immediately.

Italian Flavour Chicken Breasts with Roma Tomatoes

Prep time: 10 minutes | Cook time: 60 minutes | Serves 8

1.4 kg chicken breasts, bone-in
1 teaspoon minced fresh basil
1 teaspoon minced fresh rosemary
2 tablespoons minced fresh parsley
1 teaspoon cayenne pepper
½ teaspoon salt
½ teaspoon freshly ground black pepper
4 medium Roma tomatoes, halved
Cooking spray

1. Preheat the air fryer to 190°C. Spritz the two air fryer drawers with cooking spray. 2. Combine all the ingredients, except for the chicken breasts and tomatoes, in a large bowl. Stir to mix well. 3. Dunk the chicken breasts in the mixture and press to coat well. 4. Transfer the chicken breasts in the two preheated air fryer drawers. 5. Air fry for 25 minutes or until the internal temperature of the thickest part of the breasts reaches at least 76°C. Flip the breasts halfway through the cooking time. 6. Remove the cooked chicken breasts from the drawer and adjust the temperature to 180°C. 7. Place the tomatoes in the air fryer and spritz with cooking spray. Sprinkle with a touch of salt and cook for 10 minutes or until tender. Shake the drawer halfway through the cooking time. 8. Serve the tomatoes with chicken breasts on a large serving plate.

Harissa-Rubbed Chicken

Prep time: 30 minutes | Cook time: 21 minutes | Serves 4

Harissa:
120 ml olive oil
6 cloves garlic, minced
2 tablespoons smoked paprika
1 tablespoon ground coriander
1 tablespoon ground cumin
1 teaspoon ground caraway

1 teaspoon kosher salt
½ to 1 teaspoon cayenne pepper
Chickens:
120 g yogurt
2 small chickens, any
giblets removed, split in half
lengthwise

1. For the harissa: In a medium microwave-safe bowl, combine the oil, garlic, paprika, coriander, cumin, caraway, salt, and cayenne. Microwave on high for 1 minute, stirring halfway through the cooking time. (You can also heat this on the stovetop until the oil is hot and bubbling. Or, if you must use your air fryer for everything, cook it in the air fryer at 180ºC for 5 to 6 minutes, or until the paste is heated through.) 2. For the chicken: In a small bowl, combine 1 to 2 tablespoons harissa and the yogurt. Whisk until well combined. Place the chicken halves in a resealable plastic bag and pour the marinade over. Seal the bag and massage until all of the pieces are thoroughly coated. Marinate at room temperature for 30 minutes or in the refrigerator for up to 24 hours. 3. Arrange the hen halves in a single layer in the two air fryer drawers. Set the air fryer to 200ºC for 20 minutes. Use a meat thermometer to ensure the chickens have reached an internal temperature of 76ºC.

Wild Rice and Kale Stuffed Chicken Thighs

Prep time: 10 minutes | Cook time: 22 minutes | Serves 4

4 boneless, skinless chicken
thighs
250 g cooked wild rice
35 g chopped kale
2 garlic cloves, minced

1 teaspoon salt
Juice of 1 lemon
100 g crumbled feta
Olive oil cooking spray
1 tablespoon olive oi

1. Preheat the air fryer to 192ºC. 2. Place the chicken thighs between two pieces of plastic wrap, and using a meat mallet or a rolling pin, pound them out to about ¼-inch thick. 3. In a medium bowl, combine the rice, kale, garlic, salt, and lemon juice and mix well. 4. Place a quarter of the rice mixture into the middle of each chicken thigh, then sprinkle 2 tablespoons of feta over the filling. 5. Spray the two air fryer drawers with olive oil cooking spray. 6. Fold the sides of the chicken thigh over the filling, and then gently place each of them seam-side down into the two air fryer drawers. Brush each stuffed chicken thigh with olive oil. 7. Roast the stuffed chicken thighs for 12 minutes, then turn them over and cook for an additional 10 minutes, or until the internal temperature reaches 76ºC.

Chicken Wings with Piri Piri Sauce

Prep time: 30 minutes | Cook time: 30 minutes | Serves 6

12 chicken wings
45 g butter, melted
1 teaspoon onion powder
½ teaspoon cumin powder
1 teaspoon garlic paste
Sauce:
60 g piri piri peppers, stemmed

and chopped
1 tablespoon pimiento, seeded
and minced
1 garlic clove, chopped
2 tablespoons fresh lemon juice
⅓ teaspoon sea salt
½ teaspoon tarragon

1. Steam the chicken wings using a steamer drawer that is placed over a saucepan with boiling water; reduce the heat. 2. Now, steam the wings for 10 minutes over a moderate heat. Toss the wings with butter, onion powder, cumin powder, and garlic paste. 3. Let the chicken wings cool to room temperature. Then, refrigerate them for 45 to 50 minutes. 4. Roast in the preheated air fryer at 170ºC for 25 to 30 minutes; make sure to flip them halfway through. 5. While the chicken wings are cooking, prepare the sauce by mixing all of the sauce ingredients in a food processor. Toss the wings with prepared Piri Piri Sauce and serve.

Stuffed Chicken Florentine

Prep time: 10 minutes | Cook time: 20 minutes | Serves 4

3 tablespoons pine nuts
40 g frozen spinach, thawed
and squeezed dry
75 g ricotta cheese
2 tablespoons grated Parmesan
cheese
3 cloves garlic, minced

Salt and freshly ground black
pepper, to taste
4 small boneless, skinless
chicken breast halves (about
680 g)
8 slices bacon

1. In a large bowl, combine the spinach, ricotta, Parmesan, and garlic. Season to taste with salt and pepper and stir well until thoroughly combined. 2. Using a sharp knife, cut into the chicken breasts, slicing them across and opening them up like a book, but be careful not to cut them all the way through. Sprinkle the chicken with salt and pepper. 3. Spoon equal amounts of the spinach mixture into the chicken, then fold the top of the chicken breast back over the top of the stuffing. Wrap each chicken breast with 2 slices of bacon. 4. Air fry the chicken for 18 to 20 minutes in zone 1 drawer until the bacon is crisp and a thermometer inserted into the thickest part of the chicken registers 76ºC. 5. Place the pine nuts in a small pan and set in the zone 2 air fryer drawer. Air fry at 200ºC for 2 to 3 minutes until toasted. Remove the pine nuts to a mixing bowl.

Chapter 4 Beef, Pork, and Lamb

Chapter 4 Beef, Pork, and Lamb

Chorizo and Beef Burger

Prep time: 10 minutes | Cook time: 15 minutes | Serves 4

340 g 80/20 beef mince
110 g Mexican-style chorizo crumb
60 ml chopped onion
5 slices pickled jalapeños,
chopped
2 teaspoons chili powder
1 teaspoon minced garlic
¼ teaspoon cumin

1. In a large bowl, mix all ingredients. Divide the mixture into four sections and form them into burger patties. 2. Place burger patties into the two air fryer drawers. 3. Adjust the temperature to 192°C and air fry for 15 minutes. 4. Flip the patties halfway through the cooking time. Serve warm.

Spicy Bavette Steak with Zhoug

Prep time: 30 minutes | Cook time: 8 minutes | Serves 4

Marinade and Steak:
120 ml dark beer or orange juice
60 ml fresh lemon juice
3 cloves garlic, minced
2 tablespoons extra-virgin olive oil
2 tablespoons Sriracha
2 tablespoons brown sugar
2 teaspoons ground cumin
2 teaspoons smoked paprika
1 tablespoon coarse or flaky salt
1 teaspoon black pepper
680 g bavette or skirt steak, trimmed and cut into 3 pieces
Zhoug:
235 ml packed fresh coriander leaves
2 cloves garlic, peeled
2 jalapeño or green chiles, stemmed and coarsely chopped
½ teaspoon ground cumin
¼ teaspoon ground coriander
¼ teaspoon coarse or flaky salt
2 to 4 tablespoons extra-virgin olive oil

1. For the marinade and steak: In a small bowl, whisk together the beer, lemon juice, garlic, olive oil, Sriracha, brown sugar, cumin, paprika, salt, and pepper. Place the steak in a large resealable plastic bag. Pour the marinade over the steak, seal the bag, and massage the steak to coat. Marinate in the refrigerator for 1 hour or up to 24 hours, turning the bag occasionally. 2. Meanwhile, for the zhoug: In a food processor, combine the coriander, garlic, jalapeños, cumin, coriander, and salt. Process until finely chopped. Add 2 tablespoons olive oil and pulse to form a loose paste, adding up to 2 tablespoons more olive oil if needed. Transfer the zhoug to a glass container. Cover and store in the refrigerator until 30 minutes before serving if marinating more than 1 hour. 3. Remove the steak from the marinade and discard the marinade. Place the steak in the zone 1 air fryer drawer and set the temperature to 204°C for 8 minutes. Use a meat thermometer to ensure the steak has reached an internal temperature of 64°C (for medium). 4. Transfer the steak to a cutting board and let rest for 5 minutes. Slice the steak across the grain and serve with the zhoug.

Cinnamon-Beef Kofta

Prep time: 10 minutes | Cook time: 13 minutes | Makes 12 koftas

680 g lean beef mince
1 teaspoon onion granules
¾ teaspoon ground cinnamon
¾ teaspoon ground dried turmeric
1 teaspoon ground cumin
¾ teaspoon salt
¼ teaspoon cayenne
12 (3½- to 4-inch-long) cinnamon sticks
Cooking spray

1. Preheat the air fryer to 192°C. Spritz the two air fryer drawers with cooking spray. 2. Combine all the ingredients, except for the cinnamon sticks, in a large bowl. Toss to mix well. 3. Divide and shape the mixture into 12 balls, then wrap each ball around each cinnamon stick and leave a quarter of the length uncovered. 4. Arrange the beef-cinnamon sticks in the preheated air fryer and spritz with cooking spray. 5. Air fry for 13 minutes or until the beef is browned. Flip the sticks halfway through. 6. Serve immediately.

Spice-Rubbed Pork Loin

Prep time: 5 minutes | Cook time: 20 minutes | Serves 6

1 teaspoon paprika
½ teaspoon ground cumin
½ teaspoon chili powder
½ teaspoon garlic powder
2 tablespoons coconut oil
1 (680 g) boneless pork loin
½ teaspoon salt
¼ teaspoon ground black pepper

1. In a small bowl, mix paprika, cumin, chili powder, and garlic powder. 2. Drizzle coconut oil over pork. Sprinkle pork loin with salt and pepper, then rub spice mixture evenly on all sides. 3. Place pork loin into the two ungreased air fryer drawer. Adjust the temperature to 204°C and air fry for 20 minutes, turning pork halfway through cooking. Pork loin will be browned and have an internal temperature of at least 64°C when done. Serve warm.

Green Pepper Cheeseburgers

Prep time: 5 minutes | Cook time: 30 minutes | Serves 4

2 green peppers
680 g 85% lean beef mince
1 clove garlic, minced
1 teaspoon salt
½ teaspoon freshly ground

black pepper
4 slices Cheddar cheese (about 85 g)
4 large lettuce leaves

1. Preheat the air fryer to 204°C. 2. Arrange the peppers in the drawer of the air fryer. Pausing halfway through the cooking time to turn the peppers, air fry for 20 minutes, or until they are softened and beginning to char. Transfer the peppers to a large bowl and cover with a plate. When cool enough to handle, peel off the skin, remove the seeds and stems, and slice into strips. Set aside. 3. Meanwhile, in a large bowl, combine the beef with the garlic, salt, and pepper. Shape the beef into 4 patties. 4. Lower the heat on the air fryer to 182°C. Arrange the burgers in a single layer in the two drawers of the air fryer. Pausing halfway through the cooking time to turn the burgers, air fry for 10 minutes, or until a thermometer inserted into the thickest part registers 72°C. 5. Top the burgers with the cheese slices and continue baking for a minute or two, just until the cheese has melted. Serve the burgers on a lettuce leaf topped with the roasted peppers.

Bo Luc Lac

Prep time: 50 minutes | Cook time: 8 minutes | Serves 4

For the Meat:
2 teaspoons soy sauce
4 garlic cloves, minced
1 teaspoon coarse or flaky salt
2 teaspoons sugar
¼ teaspoon ground black pepper
1 teaspoon toasted sesame oil
680 g top rump steak, cut into 1-inch cubes
Cooking spray
For the Salad:
1 head butterhead lettuce, leaves separated and torn into large pieces
60 ml fresh mint leaves

120 ml halved baby plum tomatoes
½ red onion, halved and thinly sliced
2 tablespoons apple cider vinegar
1 garlic clove, minced
2 teaspoons sugar
¼ teaspoon coarse or flaky salt
¼ teaspoon ground black pepper
2 tablespoons vegetable oil
For Serving:
Lime wedges, for garnish
Coarse salt and freshly cracked black pepper, to taste

1. Combine the ingredients for the meat, except for the steak, in a large bowl. Stir to mix well. 2. Dunk the steak cubes in the bowl and press to coat. Wrap the bowl in plastic and marinate under room temperature for at least 30 minutes. 3. Preheat the air fryer to 232°C. Spritz the two air fryer drawers with cooking spray. 4. Discard the marinade and transfer the steak cubes in the two preheated air fryer drawers. 5. Air fry for 4 minutes or until the steak cubes are lightly browned but still have a little pink. Shake the drawers halfway through the cooking time. 6. Meanwhile, combine the ingredients for the salad in a separate large bowl. Toss

to mix well. 7. Pour the salad in a large serving bowl and top with the steak cubes. Squeeze the lime wedges over and sprinkle with salt and black pepper before serving.

Honey-Baked Pork Loin

Prep time: 30 minutes | Cook time: 22 to 25 minutes

| Serves 6

60 ml honey
60 ml freshly squeezed lemon juice
2 tablespoons soy sauce

1 teaspoon garlic powder
1 (900 g) pork loin
2 tablespoons vegetable oil

1. In a medium bowl, whisk together the honey, lemon juice, soy sauce, and garlic powder. Reserve half of the mixture for basting during cooking. 2. Cut 5 slits in the pork loin and transfer it to a resealable bag. Add the remaining honey mixture. Seal the bag and refrigerate to marinate for at least 2 hours. 3. Preheat the air fryer to 204°C. Line the two air fryer drawers with parchment paper. 4. Remove the pork from the marinade, and place it on the parchment. Spritz with oil, then baste with the reserved marinade. 5. Cook for 15 minutes. Flip the pork, baste with more marinade and spritz with oil again. Cook for 7 to 10 minutes more until the internal temperature reaches 64°C. Let rest for 5 minutes before serving.

Five-Spice Pork Belly

Prep time: 10 minutes | Cook time: 17 minutes | Serves 4

450 g unsalted pork belly
2 teaspoons Chinese five-spice powder
Sauce:
1 tablespoon coconut oil
1 (1-inch) piece fresh ginger, peeled and grated

2 cloves garlic, minced
120 ml beef or chicken stock
¼ to 120 ml liquid or powdered sweetener
3 tablespoons wheat-free tamari
1 spring onion, sliced, plus more for garnish

1. Spray the two air fryer drawers with avocado oil. Preheat the air fryer to 204°C. 2. Cut the pork belly into ½-inch-thick slices and season well on all sides with the five-spice powder. Place the slices in a single layer in the two air fryer drawers and cook for 8 minutes, or until cooked to your liking, flipping halfway through. 3. While the pork belly cooks, make the sauce: Heat the coconut oil in a small saucepan over medium heat. Add the ginger and garlic and sauté for 1 minute, or until fragrant. Add the stock, sweetener, and tamari and simmer for 10 to 15 minutes, until thickened. Add the spring onion and cook for another minute, until the spring onion is softened. Taste and adjust the seasoning to your liking. 4. Transfer the pork belly to a large bowl. Pour the sauce over the pork belly and coat well. Place the pork belly slices on a serving platter and garnish with sliced spring onions. 5. Best served fresh. Store leftovers in an airtight container in the fridge for up to 4 days. Reheat in a preheated 204°C air fryer for 3 minutes, or until heated through.

Sausage-Stuffed Peppers

Prep time: 15 minutes | Cook time: 28 to 30 minutes
| Serves 6

Avocado oil spray
230 g Italian-seasoned sausage, casings removed
120 ml chopped mushrooms
60 ml diced onion
1 teaspoon Italian seasoning
Sea salt and freshly ground

black pepper, to taste
235 ml keto-friendly marinara sauce
3 peppers, halved and seeded
85 g low-moisture Mozzarella or other melting cheese, shredded

1. Spray a large skillet with oil and place it over medium-high heat. Add the sausage and cook for 5 minutes, breaking up the meat with a wooden spoon. Add the mushrooms, onion, and Italian seasoning, and season with salt and pepper. Cook for 5 minutes more. Stir in the marinara sauce and cook until heated through. 2. Scoop the sausage filling into the pepper halves. 3. Set the air fryer to 176ºC. Arrange the peppers in a single layer in the two air fryer drawers. Air fry for 15 minutes. 4. Top the stuffed peppers with the cheese and air fry for 3 to 5 minutes more, until the cheese is melted and the peppers are tender.

Pigs in a Blanket and Currywurst

Prep time: 25 minutes | Cook time: 12 minutes | Serves 6

Pigs in a Blanket:
120 ml shredded Mozzarella cheese
2 tablespoons blanched finely ground almond flour
30 g full-fat cream cheese
2 (110 g) beef smoked sausage, cut in two
½ teaspoon sesame seeds
Currywurst:

235 ml tomato sauce
2 tablespoons cider vinegar
2 teaspoons curry powder
2 teaspoons sweet paprika
1 teaspoon sugar
¼ teaspoon cayenne pepper
1 small onion, diced
450 g bratwurst, sliced diagonally into 1-inch pieces

Make the Pigs in a Blanket (zone 1 drawer): 1. Place Mozzarella, almond flour, and cream cheese in a large microwave-safe bowl. Microwave for 45 seconds and stir until smooth. Roll dough into a ball and cut in half. 2. Press each half out into a 4 × 5-inch rectangle. Roll one sausage up in each dough half and press seams closed. Sprinkle the top with sesame seeds. 3. Place each wrapped sausage into the zone 1 air fryer drawer. 4. Adjust the temperature to 204ºC and air fry for 7 minutes. 5. The outside will be golden when completely cooked. Serve immediately.
Make the Currywurst (zone 2 drawer): 1. In a large bowl, combine the tomato sauce, vinegar, curry powder, paprika, sugar, and cayenne. Whisk until well combined. Stir in the onion and bratwurst. 2. Transfer the mixture to a baking pan. Place the pan in the zone 2 air fryer drawer. Set the temperature to 204ºC for 12 minutes, or until the sausage is heated through and the sauce is bubbling.

Kielbasa and Cabbage

Prep time: 10 minutes | Cook time: 20 to 25 minutes
| Serves 4

450 g smoked kielbasa sausage, sliced into ½-inch pieces
1 head cabbage, very coarsely chopped
½ brown onion, chopped
2 cloves garlic, chopped

2 tablespoons olive oil
½ teaspoon salt
½ teaspoon freshly ground black pepper
60 ml water

1. Preheat the zone 1 air fryer drawer to 204ºC. 2. In a large bowl, combine the sausage, cabbage, onion, garlic, olive oil, salt, and black pepper. Toss until thoroughly combined. 3. Transfer the mixture to the zone 1 drawer of the air fryer and pour the water over the top. Pausing two or three times during the cooking time to shake the drawer, air fry for 20 to 25 minutes, until the sausage is browned and the vegetables are tender.

Kielbasa Sausage with Pineapple and Kheema Meatloaf

Prep time: 25 minutes | Cook time: 15 minutes |
Serves 6 to 8

Kielbasa Sausage with Pineapple:
340 g kielbasa sausage, cut into ½-inch slices
1 (230 g) can pineapple chunks in juice, drained
235 ml pepper chunks
1 tablespoon barbecue seasoning
1 tablespoon soy sauce
Cooking spray
Kheema Meatloaf:
450 g 85% lean beef mince

2 large eggs, lightly beaten
235 ml diced brown onion
60 ml chopped fresh coriander
1 tablespoon minced fresh ginger
1 tablespoon minced garlic
2 teaspoons garam masala
1 teaspoon coarse or flaky salt
1 teaspoon ground turmeric
1 teaspoon cayenne pepper
½ teaspoon ground cinnamon
⅛ teaspoon ground cardamom

Make the Kielbasa Sausage with Pineapple (zone 1 drawer): 1. Preheat the air fryer to 200ºC. Spritz the zone 1 air fryer drawer with cooking spray. 2. Combine all the ingredients in a large bowl. Toss to mix well. 3. Pour the sausage mixture in the preheated zone 1 air fryer drawer. 4. Air fry for 10 minutes or until the sausage is lightly browned and the pepper and pineapple are soft. Shake the drawer halfway through. Serve immediately.
Make the Kheema Meatloaf (zone 2 drawer): 1. In a large bowl, gently mix the beef mince, eggs, onion, coriander, ginger, garlic, garam masala, salt, turmeric, cayenne, cinnamon, and cardamom until thoroughly combined. 2. Place the seasoned meat in a baking pan. Place the pan in the zone 2 air fryer drawer. Set the temperature to 176ºC for 15 minutes. Use a meat thermometer to ensure the meat loaf has reached an internal temperature of 72ºC (medium). 3. Drain the fat and liquid from the pan and let stand for 5 minutes before slicing. 4. Slice and serve hot.

Sweet and Spicy Country-Style Ribs

Prep time: 10 minutes | Cook time: 25 minutes | Serves 4

2 tablespoons brown sugar	1 teaspoon coarse or flaky salt
2 tablespoons smoked paprika	1 teaspoon black pepper
1 teaspoon garlic powder	¼ to ½ teaspoon cayenne
1 teaspoon onion granules	pepper
1 teaspoon mustard powder	680 g boneless pork steaks
1 teaspoon ground cumin	235 ml barbecue sauce

1. In a small bowl, stir together the brown sugar, paprika, garlic powder, onion granules, mustard powder, cumin, salt, black pepper, and cayenne. Mix until well combined. 2. Pat the ribs dry with a paper towel. Generously sprinkle the rub evenly over both sides of the ribs and rub in with your fingers. 3. Place the ribs in the two air fryer drawers. Set the air fryer to 176ºC for 15 minutes. Turn the ribs and brush with 120 ml of the barbecue sauce. Cook for an additional 10 minutes. Use a meat thermometer to ensure the pork has reached an internal temperature of 64ºC. 4. Serve with remaining barbecue sauce.

Bacon and Cheese Stuffed Pork Chops

Prep time: 10 minutes | Cook time: 12 minutes | Serves 4

15 g plain pork scratchings, finely crushed	crumbled
	4 (110 g) boneless pork chops
120 ml shredded sharp Cheddar cheese	½ teaspoon salt
	¼ teaspoon ground black
4 slices cooked bacon,	pepper

1. In a small bowl, mix pork scratchings, Cheddar, and bacon. 2. Make a 3-inch slit in the side of each pork chop and stuff with ¼ pork rind mixture. Sprinkle each side of pork chops with salt and pepper. 3. Place pork chops into the two ungreased air fryer drawers, stuffed side up. Adjust the temperature to 204ºC and air fry for 12 minutes. Pork chops will be browned and have an internal temperature of at least 64ºC when done. Serve warm.

Mojito Lamb Chops

Prep time: 30 minutes | Cook time: 5 minutes | Serves 2

Marinade:	2 teaspoons fine sea salt
2 teaspoons grated lime zest	½ teaspoon ground black
120 ml lime juice	pepper
60 ml avocado oil	4 (1-inch-thick) lamb chops
60 ml chopped fresh mint leaves	Sprigs of fresh mint, for garnish (optional)
4 cloves garlic, roughly chopped	Lime slices, for serving (optional)

1. Make the marinade: Place all the ingredients for the marinade in a food processor or blender and purée until mostly smooth with a few small chunks. Transfer half of the marinade to a shallow dish and set the other half aside for serving. Add the lamb to the shallow dish, cover, and place in the refrigerator to marinate for at least 2 hours or overnight. 2. Spray the two air fryer drawers with avocado oil. Preheat the air fryer to 200ºC. 3. Remove the chops from the marinade and place them in the two air fryer drawers. Air fry for 5 minutes, or until the internal temperature reaches 64ºC for medium doneness. 4. Allow the chops to rest for 10 minutes before serving with the rest of the marinade as a sauce. Garnish with fresh mint leaves and serve with lime slices, if desired. Best served fresh.

Garlic Butter Steak Bites

Prep time: 5 minutes | Cook time: 16 minutes | Serves 3

Oil, for spraying	sauce
450 g boneless steak, cut into	½ teaspoon granulated garlic
1-inch pieces	½ teaspoon salt
2 tablespoons olive oil	¼ teaspoon freshly ground
1 teaspoon Worcestershire	black pepper

1. Preheat the air fryer to 204ºC. Line the two air fryer drawers with parchment and spray lightly with oil. 2. In a medium bowl, combine the steak, olive oil, Worcestershire sauce, garlic, salt, and black pepper and toss until evenly coated. 3. Place the steak in a single layer in the two prepared drawers. 4. Cook for 10 to 16 minutes, flipping every 3 to 4 minutes. The total cooking time will depend on the thickness of the meat and your preferred doneness. If you want it well done, it may take up to 5 additional minutes.

Air Fryer Chicken-Fried Steak

Prep time: 5 minutes | Cook time: 20 minutes | Serves 4

450 g beef braising steak	2 medium egg whites
700 ml low-fat milk, divided	235 ml gluten-free breadcrumbs
1 teaspoon dried thyme	120 ml coconut flour
1 teaspoon dried rosemary	1 tablespoon Cajun seasoning

1. In a bowl, marinate the steak in 475 ml of milk for 30 to 45 minutes. 2. Remove the steak from milk, shake off the excess liquid, and season with the thyme and rosemary. Discard the milk. 3. In a shallow bowl, beat the egg whites with the remaining 235 ml of milk. 4. In a separate shallow bowl, combine the breadcrumbs, coconut flour, and seasoning. 5. Dip the steak in the egg white mixture then dredge in the breadcrumb mixture, coating well. 6. Place the steak in the zone 1 drawer of an air fryer. 7. Set the temperature to 200ºC, close, and cook for 10 minutes. 8. Open the air fryer, turn the steaks, close, and cook for 10 minutes. Let rest for 5 minutes.

Sumptuous Pizza Tortilla Rolls

Prep time: 10 minutes | Cook time: 6 minutes | Serves 4

1 teaspoon butter	8 flour tortillas
½ medium onion, slivered	8 thin slices wafer-thinham
½ red or green pepper, julienned	24 pepperoni slices
110 g fresh white mushrooms, chopped	235 ml shredded Mozzarella cheese
120 ml pizza sauce	Cooking spray

1. Preheat the air fryer to 200°C. 2. Put butter, onions, pepper, and mushrooms in a baking pan. Bake in the preheated air fryer for 3 minutes. Stir and cook 3 to 4 minutes longer until just crisp and tender. Remove pan and set aside. 3. To assemble rolls, spread about 2 teaspoons of pizza sauce on one half of each tortilla. Top with a slice of ham and 3 slices of pepperoni. Divide sautéed vegetables among tortillas and top with cheese. 4. Roll up tortillas, secure with toothpicks if needed, and spray with oil. 5. Put the rolls in the two air fryer drawers and air fry for 4 minutes. Turn and air fry 4 minutes, until heated through and lightly browned. 6. Serve immediately.

Blue Cheese Steak Salad

Prep time: 30 minutes | Cook time: 22 minutes | Serves 4

2 tablespoons balsamic vinegar	180 ml extra-virgin olive oil
2 tablespoons red wine vinegar	450 g boneless rump steak
1 tablespoon Dijon mustard	Avocado oil spray
1 tablespoon granulated sweetener	1 small red onion, cut into ¼-inch-thick rounds
1 teaspoon minced garlic	170 g baby spinach
Sea salt and freshly ground black pepper, to taste	120 ml cherry tomatoes, halved
	85 g blue cheese, crumbled

1. In a blender, combine the balsamic vinegar, red wine vinegar, Dijon mustard, sweetener, and garlic. Season with salt and pepper and process until smooth. With the blender running, drizzle in the olive oil. Process until well combined. Transfer to a jar with a tight-fitting lid, and refrigerate until ready to serve (it will keep for up to 2 weeks). 2. Season the steak with salt and pepper and let sit at room temperature for at least 45 minutes, time permitting. 3. Set the zone 1 air fryer drawer to 204°C. Spray the steak with oil and place it in the zone 1 air fryer drawer. Spray the onion slices with oil and place them in the zone 2 air fryer drawer. 4. In zone 1, air fry for 6 minutes. Flip the steak and spray it with more oil. Air fry for 6 minutes more for medium-rare or until the steak is done to your liking. 5. In zone 2, cook at 204°C for 5 minutes. Flip the onion slices and spray them with more oil. Air fry for 5 minutes more. 6. Transfer the steak to a plate, tent with a piece of aluminum foil, and allow it to rest. Slice the steak diagonally into thin strips. Place the spinach, cherry tomatoes, onion slices, and steak in a large bowl. Toss with the desired amount of dressing. Sprinkle with crumbled blue cheese and serve.

Bacon-Wrapped Vegetable Kebabs

Prep time: 10 minutes | Cook time: 10 to 12 minutes | Serves 4

110 g mushrooms, sliced	Avocado oil spray
1 small courgette, sliced	Sea salt and freshly ground black pepper, to taste
12 baby plum tomatoes	
110 g sliced bacon, halved	

1. Stack 3 mushroom slices, 1 courgette slice, and 1 tomato. Wrap a bacon strip around the vegetables and thread them onto a skewer. Repeat with the remaining vegetables and bacon. Spray with oil and sprinkle with salt and pepper. 2. Set the air fryer to 204°C. Place the skewers in the two air fryer drawers in a single layer and air fry for 5 minutes. Flip the skewers and cook for 5 to 7 minutes more, until the bacon is crispy and the vegetables are tender. 3. Serve warm.

Sausage and Cauliflower Arancini

Prep time: 30 minutes | Cook time: 28 to 32 minutes | Serves 6

Avocado oil spray	85 g cream cheese
170 g Italian-seasoned sausage, casings removed	110 g Cheddar cheese, shredded
60 ml diced onion	1 large egg
1 teaspoon minced garlic	120 ml finely ground blanched almond flour
1 teaspoon dried thyme	60 ml finely grated Parmesan cheese
Sea salt and freshly ground black pepper, to taste	Keto-friendly marinara sauce, for serving
120 ml cauliflower rice	

1. Spray a large skillet with oil and place it over medium-high heat. Once the skillet is hot, put the sausage in the skillet and cook for 7 minutes, breaking up the meat with the back of a spoon. 2. Reduce the heat to medium and add the onion. Cook for 5 minutes, then add the garlic, thyme, and salt and pepper to taste. Cook for 1 minute more. 3. Add the cauliflower rice and cream cheese to the skillet. Cook for 7 minutes, stirring frequently, until the cream cheese melts and the cauliflower is tender. 4. Remove the skillet from the heat and stir in the Cheddar cheese. Using a cookie scoop, form the mixture into 1½-inch balls. Place the balls on a parchment paper-lined baking sheet. Freeze for 30 minutes. 5. Place the egg in a shallow bowl and beat it with a fork. In a separate bowl, stir together the almond flour and Parmesan cheese. 6. Dip the cauliflower balls into the egg, then coat them with the almond flour mixture, gently pressing the mixture to the balls to adhere. 7. Set the air fryer to 204°C. Spray the cauliflower rice balls with oil, and arrange them in a single layer in the two air fryer drawers. Air fry for 5 minutes. Flip the rice balls and spray them with more oil. Air fry for 3 to 7 minutes longer, until the balls are golden brown. 8. Serve warm with marinara sauce.

Nigerian Peanut-Crusted Bavette Steak

Prep time: 30 minutes | Cook time: 8 minutes | Serves 4

Suya Spice Mix:
60 ml dry-roasted peanuts
1 teaspoon cumin seeds
1 teaspoon garlic powder
1 teaspoon smoked paprika
½ teaspoon ground ginger
1 teaspoon coarse or flaky salt
½ teaspoon cayenne pepper
Steak:
450 g bavette or skirt steak
2 tablespoons vegetable oil

1. For the spice mix: In a clean coffee grinder or spice mill, combine the peanuts and cumin seeds. Process until you get a coarse powder. (Do not overprocess or you will wind up with peanut butter! Alternatively, you can grind the cumin with 80 ml ready-made peanut powder instead of the peanuts.) 2. Pour the peanut mixture into a small bowl, add the garlic powder, paprika, ginger, salt, and cayenne, and stir to combine. This recipe makes about 120 ml suya spice mix. Store leftovers in an airtight container in a cool, dry place for up to 1 month. 3. For the steak: Cut the steak into ½-inch-thick slices, cutting against the grain and at a slight angle. Place the beef strips in a resealable plastic bag and add the oil and 2½ to 3 tablespoons of the spice mixture. Seal the bag and massage to coat all of the meat with the oil and spice mixture. Marinate at room temperature for 30 minutes or in the refrigerator for up to 24 hours. 4. Place the beef strips in the zone 1 air fryer drawer. Set the temperature to 204ºC for 8 minutes, turning the strips halfway through the cooking time. 5. Transfer the meat to a serving platter. Sprinkle with additional spice mix, if desired.

Italian Sausages with Peppers and Teriyaki Rump Steak with Broccoli

Prep time: 10 minutes | Cook time: 28 minutes | Serves 7

Italian Sausages with Peppers:
1 medium onion, thinly sliced
1 yellow or orange pepper, thinly sliced
1 red pepper, thinly sliced
60 ml avocado oil or melted coconut oil
1 teaspoon fine sea salt
6 Italian-seasoned sausages
Dijon mustard, for serving (optional)

Teriyaki Rump Steak with Broccoli:
230 g rump steak
80 ml teriyaki marinade
1½ teaspoons sesame oil
½ head broccoli, cut into florets
2 red peppers, sliced
Fine sea salt and ground black pepper, to taste
Cooking spray

Make the Italian Sausages with Peppers (zone 1 drawer): 1. Preheat the air fryer to 204ºC. 2. Place the onion and peppers in a large bowl. Drizzle with the oil and toss well to coat the veggies. Season with the salt. 3. Place the onion and peppers in a pie pan and cook in the air fryer for 8 minutes, stirring halfway through. Remove from the air fryer and set aside. 4. Spray the zone 1 air fryer drawer with avocado oil. Place the sausages in the zone 1 air fryer drawer and air fry for 20 minutes, or until crispy and golden brown. During the last minute or two of cooking, add the onion and peppers to the drawer with the sausages to warm them through. 5. Place the onion and peppers on a serving platter and arrange the sausages on top. Serve Dijon mustard on the side, if desired. 6. Store leftovers in an airtight container in the fridge for up to 7 days or in the freezer for up to a month. Reheat in a preheated 200ºC air fryer for 3 minutes, or until heated through.

Make the Teriyaki Rump Steak with Broccoli (zone 2 drawer): 1. Toss the rump steak in a large bowl with teriyaki marinade. Wrap the bowl in plastic and refrigerate to marinate for at least an hour. 2. Preheat the air fryer to 204ºC and spritz with cooking spray. 3. Discard the marinade and transfer the steak in the preheated zone 2 air fryer drawer. Spritz with cooking spray. 4. Air fry for 13 minutes or until well browned. Flip the steak halfway through. 5. Meanwhile, heat the sesame oil in a nonstick skillet over medium heat. Add the broccoli and red pepper. Sprinkle with salt and ground black pepper. Sauté for 5 minutes or until the broccoli is tender. 6. Transfer the air fried rump steak on a plate and top with the sautéed broccoli and pepper. Serve hot.

Kheema Burgers

Prep time: 15 minutes | Cook time: 12 minutes | Serves 4

Burgers:
450 g 85% lean beef mince or lamb mince
2 large eggs, lightly beaten
1 medium brown onion, diced
60 ml chopped fresh coriander
1 tablespoon minced fresh ginger
3 cloves garlic, minced
2 teaspoons garam masala
1 teaspoon ground turmeric
½ teaspoon ground cinnamon
⅛ teaspoon ground cardamom
1 teaspoon coarse or flaky salt
1 teaspoon cayenne pepper
Raita Sauce:
235 ml grated cucumber
120 ml sour cream
¼ teaspoon coarse or flaky salt
¼ teaspoon black pepper
For Serving:
4 lettuce leaves, hamburger buns, or naan breads

1. For the burgers: In a large bowl, combine the beef mince, eggs, onion, coriander, ginger, garlic, garam masala, turmeric, cinnamon, cardamom, salt, and cayenne. Gently mix until ingredients are thoroughly combined. 2. Divide the meat into four portions and form into round patties. Make a slight depression in the middle of each patty with your thumb to prevent them from puffing up into a dome shape while cooking. 3. Place the patties in the zone 1 air fryer drawer. Set the temperature to 176ºC for 12 minutes. Use a meat thermometer to ensure the burgers have reached an internal temperature of 72ºC (for medium). 4. Meanwhile, for the sauce: In a small bowl, combine the cucumber, sour cream, salt, and pepper. 5. To serve: Place the burgers on the lettuce, buns, or naan and top with the sauce.

Rosemary Ribeye Steaks and Mongolian-Style Beef

Prep time: 20 minutes | Cook time: 15 minutes | Serves 6

Rosemary Ribeye Steaks:
60 ml butter
1 clove garlic, minced
Salt and ground black pepper, to taste
1½ tablespoons balsamic vinegar
60 ml rosemary, chopped
2 ribeye steaks
Mongolian-Style Beef:
Oil, for spraying
60 ml cornflour
450 g bavette or skirt steak, thinly sliced
180 ml packed light brown sugar
120 ml soy sauce
2 teaspoons toasted sesame oil
1 tablespoon minced garlic
½ teaspoon ground ginger
120 ml water
Cooked white rice or ramen noodles, for serving

Make the Rosemary Ribeye Steaks (zone 1 drawer): 1. Melt the butter in a skillet over medium heat. Add the garlic and fry until fragrant. 2. Remove the skillet from the heat and add the salt, pepper, and vinegar. Allow it to cool. 3. Add the rosemary, then pour the mixture into a Ziploc bag. 4. Put the ribeye steaks in the bag and shake well, coating the meat well. Refrigerate for an hour, then allow to sit for a further twenty minutes. 5. Preheat the zone 1 air fryer drawer to 204°C. 6. Air fry the ribeye steaks for 15 minutes. 7. Take care when removing the steaks from the air fryer and plate up. 8. Serve immediately.

Make the Mongolian-Style Beef (zone 2 drawer): 1. Line the zone 2 air fryer drawer with parchment and spray lightly with oil. 2. Place the cornflour in a bowl and dredge the steak until evenly coated. Shake off any excess cornflour. 3. Place the steak in the prepared drawer and spray lightly with oil. 4. Roast at 200°C for 5 minutes, flip, and cook for another 5 minutes. 5. In a small saucepan, combine the brown sugar, soy sauce, sesame oil, garlic, ginger, and water and bring to a boil over medium-high heat, stirring frequently. Remove from the heat. 6. Transfer the meat to the sauce and toss until evenly coated. Let sit for about 5 minutes so the steak absorbs the flavors. Serve with white rice or ramen noodles.

Smothered Chops

Prep time: 20 minutes | Cook time: 30 minutes | Serves 4

4 bone-in pork chops (230 g each)
2 teaspoons salt, divided
1½ teaspoons freshly ground black pepper, divided
1 teaspoon garlic powder
235 ml tomato purée
1½ teaspoons Italian seasoning
1 tablespoon sugar
1 tablespoon cornflour
120 ml chopped onion
120 ml chopped green pepper
1 to 2 tablespoons oil

1. Evenly season the pork chops with 1 teaspoon salt, 1 teaspoon pepper, and the garlic powder. 2. In a medium bowl, stir together the tomato purée, Italian seasoning, sugar, remaining 1 teaspoon of salt, and remaining ½ teaspoon of pepper. 3. In a small bowl,

whisk 180 ml water and the cornflour until blended. Stir this slurry into the tomato purée, with the onion and green pepper. Transfer to a baking pan. 4. Preheat the air fryer to 176°C. 5. Place the sauce in the fryer and cook for 10 minutes. Stir and cook for 10 minutes more. Remove the pan and keep warm. 6. Increase the air fryer temperature to 204°C. Line the two air fryer drawers with parchment paper. 7. Place the pork chops on the parchment and spritz with oil. 8. Cook for 5 minutes. Flip and spritz the chops with oil and cook for 5 minutes more, until the internal temperature reaches 64°C. Serve with the tomato mixture spooned on top.

Bacon-Wrapped Hot Dogs with Mayo-Ketchup Sauce

Prep time: 5 minutes | Cook time: 10 to 12 minutes | Serves 5

10 thin slices of bacon
5 pork hot dogs, halved
1 teaspoon cayenne pepper
Sauce:
60 ml mayonnaise
4 tablespoons ketchup
1 teaspoon rice vinegar
1 teaspoon chili powder

1. Preheat the air fryer to 200°C. 2. Arrange the slices of bacon on a clean work surface. One by one, place the halved hot dog on one end of each slice, season with cayenne pepper and wrap the hot dog with the bacon slices and secure with toothpicks as needed. 3. Place half the wrapped hot dogs in the two air fryer drawers and air fry for 10 to 12 minutes or until the bacon becomes browned and crispy. 4. Make the sauce: Stir all the ingredients for the sauce in a small bowl. Wrap the bowl in plastic and set in the refrigerator until ready to serve. 5. Transfer the hot dogs to a platter and serve hot with the sauce.

Panko Crusted Calf's Liver Strips

Prep time: 15 minutes | Cook time: 23 to 25 minutes | Serves 4

450 g sliced calf's liver, cut into ½-inch wide strips
2 eggs
2 tablespoons milk
120 ml whole wheat flour
475 ml panko breadcrumbs
Salt and ground black pepper, to taste
Cooking spray

1. Preheat the air fryer to 200°C and spritz with cooking spray. 2. Rub the calf's liver strips with salt and ground black pepper on a clean work surface. 3. Whisk the eggs with milk in a large bowl. Pour the flour in a shallow dish. Pour the panko on a separate shallow dish. 4. Dunk the liver strips in the flour, then in the egg mixture. Shake the excess off and roll the strips over the panko to coat well. 5. Arrange the liver strips in a single layer in the two preheated air fryer drawers and spritz with cooking spray. 6. Air fry for 5 minutes or until browned. Flip the strips halfway through. 7. Serve immediately.

Steaks with Walnut-Blue Cheese Butter

Prep time: 30 minutes | Cook time: 10 minutes | Serves 6

120 ml unsalted butter, at room temperature
120 ml crumbled blue cheese
2 tablespoons finely chopped walnuts
1 tablespoon minced fresh rosemary

1 teaspoon minced garlic
¼ teaspoon cayenne pepper
Sea salt and freshly ground black pepper, to taste
680 g sirloin steaks, at room temperature

1. In a medium bowl, combine the butter, blue cheese, walnuts, rosemary, garlic, and cayenne pepper and salt and black pepper to taste. Use clean hands to ensure that everything is well combined. Place the mixture on a sheet of parchment paper and form it into a log. Wrap it tightly in plastic wrap. Refrigerate for at least 2 hours or freeze for 30 minutes. 2. Season the steaks generously with salt and pepper. 3. Set the air fryer to 204°C and let it preheat for 5 minutes. 4. Place the steaks in the two drawers in a single layer and air fry for 5 minutes. Flip the steaks, and cook for 5 minutes more, until an instant-read thermometer reads 49°C for medium-rare (or as desired). 5. Transfer the steaks to a plate. Cut the butter into pieces and place the desired amount on top of the steaks. Tent a piece of aluminum foil over the steaks and allow to sit for 10 minutes before serving. 6. Store any remaining butter in a sealed container in the refrigerator for up to 2 weeks.

Meat and Rice Stuffed Peppers

Prep time: 20 minutes | Cook time: 18 minutes | Serves 4

340 g lean beef mince
110 g lean pork mince
60 ml onion, minced
1 (425 g) can finely-chopped tomatoes
1 teaspoon Worcestershire sauce
1 teaspoon barbecue seasoning
1 teaspoon honey

½ teaspoon dried basil
120 ml cooked brown rice
½ teaspoon garlic powder
½ teaspoon oregano
½ teaspoon salt
2 small peppers, cut in half, stems removed, deseeded
Cooking spray

1. Preheat the zone 1 air fryer drawer to 182°C and spritz a baking pan with cooking spray. 2. Arrange the beef, pork, and onion in the baking pan and bake in the preheated air fryer drawer for 8 minutes. Break the ground meat into chunks halfway through the cooking. 3. Meanwhile, combine the tomatoes, Worcestershire sauce, barbecue seasoning, honey, and basil in a saucepan. Stir to mix well. 4. Transfer the cooked meat mixture to a large bowl and add the cooked rice, garlic powder, oregano, salt, and 60 ml of the tomato mixture. Stir to mix well. 5. Stuff the pepper halves with the mixture, then arrange the pepper halves in the zone 1 air fryer drawer and air fry for 10 minutes or until the peppers are lightly charred. 6. Serve the stuffed peppers with the remaining tomato sauce on top.

Stuffed Beef Fillet with Feta Cheese

Prep time: 10 minutes | Cook time: 10 minutes | Serves 4

680 g beef fillet, pounded to ¼ inch thick
3 teaspoons sea salt
1 teaspoon ground black pepper
60 g creamy goat cheese

120 ml crumbled feta cheese
60 ml finely chopped onions
2 cloves garlic, minced
Cooking spray

1. Preheat the air fryer to 204°C. Spritz the two air fryer drawers with cooking spray. 2. Unfold the beef on a clean work surface. Rub the salt and pepper all over the beef to season. 3. Make the filling for the stuffed beef fillet: Combine the goat cheese, feta, onions, and garlic in a medium bowl. Stir until well blended. 4. Spoon the mixture in the center of the fillet. Roll the fillet up tightly like rolling a burrito and use some kitchen twine to tie the fillet. 5. Arrange the fillet in the two air fryer drawers and air fry for 10 minutes, flipping the fillet halfway through to ensure even cooking, or until an instant-read thermometer inserted in the center of the fillet registers 57°C for medium-rare. 6. Transfer to a platter and serve immediately.

Asian Glazed Meatballs

Prep time: 15 minutes | Cook time: 10 minutes|
Serves 4 to 6

1 large shallot, finely chopped
2 cloves garlic, minced
1 tablespoon grated fresh ginger
2 teaspoons fresh thyme, finely chopped
355 ml brown mushrooms, very finely chopped
2 tablespoons soy sauce
Freshly ground black pepper, to

taste
450 g beef mince
230 g pork mince
3 egg yolks
235 ml Thai sweet chili sauce (spring roll sauce)
60 ml toasted sesame seeds
2 spring onions, sliced

1. Combine the shallot, garlic, ginger, thyme, mushrooms, soy sauce, freshly ground black pepper, beef and pork mince, and egg yolks in a bowl and mix the ingredients together. Gently shape the mixture into 24 balls, about the size of a golf ball. 2. Preheat the air fryer to 192°C. 3. Air fry the meatballs in the two drawers for 8 minutes, turning the meatballs over halfway through the cooking time. Drizzle some of the Thai sweet chili sauce on top of each meatball and return the drawers to the air fryer, air frying for another 2 minutes. Reserve the remaining Thai sweet chili sauce for serving. 4. As soon as the meatballs are done, sprinkle with toasted sesame seeds and transfer them to a serving platter. Scatter the spring onions around and serve warm.

Minute Steak Roll-Ups

Prep time: 30 minutes | Cook time: 8 to 10 minutes | Serves 4

4 minute steaks (170 g each)	onion
1 (450 g) bottle Italian dressing	120 ml finely chopped green
1 teaspoon salt	pepper
½ teaspoon freshly ground	120 ml finely chopped
black pepper	mushrooms
120 ml finely chopped brown	1 to 2 tablespoons oil

1. In a large resealable bag or airtight storage container, combine the steaks and Italian dressing. Seal the bag and refrigerate to marinate for 2 hours. 2. Remove the steaks from the marinade and place them on a cutting board. Discard the marinade. Evenly season the steaks with salt and pepper. 3. In a small bowl, stir together the onion, pepper, and mushrooms. Sprinkle the onion mixture evenly over the steaks. Roll up the steaks, jelly roll-style, and secure with toothpicks. 4. Preheat the air fryer to 204ºC. 5. Place the steaks in the two air fryer drawers. 6. Cook for 4 minutes. Flip the steaks and spritz them with oil. Cook for 4 to 6 minutes more until the internal temperature reaches 64ºC. Let rest for 5 minutes before serving.

Bacon-Wrapped Cheese Pork

Prep time: 10 minutes | Cook time: 20 minutes | Serves 4

4 (1-inch-thick) boneless pork	cheese
chops	8 slices thin-cut bacon
2 (150 g) packages Boursin	

1. Spray the air fryer drawer with avocado oil. Preheat the air fryer to 204ºC. 2. Place one of the chops on a cutting board. With a sharp knife held parallel to the cutting board, make a 1-inch-wide incision on the top edge of the chop. Carefully cut into the chop to form a large pocket, leaving a ½-inch border along the sides and bottom. Repeat with the other 3 chops. 3. Snip the corner of a large resealable plastic bag to form a ¾-inch hole. Place the Boursin cheese in the bag and pipe the cheese into the pockets in the chops, dividing the cheese evenly among them. 4. Wrap 2 slices of bacon around each chop and secure the ends with toothpicks. Place the bacon-wrapped chops in the two air fryer drawers and cook for 10 minutes, then flip the chops and cook for another 8 to 10 minutes, until the bacon is crisp, the chops are cooked through, and the internal temperature reaches 64ºC. 5. Store leftovers in an airtight container in the refrigerator for up to 3 days. Reheat in a preheated 204ºC air fryer for 5 minutes, or until warmed through.

Goat Cheese-Stuffed Bavette Steak

Prep time: 10 minutes | Cook time: 14 minutes | Serves 6

450 g bavette or skirt steak	¼ teaspoon freshly ground
1 tablespoon avocado oil	black pepper
½ teaspoon sea salt	60 g goat cheese, crumbled
½ teaspoon garlic powder	235 ml baby spinach, chopped

1. Place the steak in a large zip-top bag or between two pieces of plastic wrap. Using a meat mallet or heavy-bottomed skillet, pound the steak to an even ¼-inch thickness. 2. Brush both sides of the steak with the avocado oil. 3. Mix the salt, garlic powder, and pepper in a small dish. Sprinkle this mixture over both sides of the steak. 4. Sprinkle the goat cheese over top, and top that with the spinach. 5. Starting at one of the long sides, roll the steak up tightly. Tie the rolled steak with kitchen string at 3-inch intervals. 6. Set the zone 1 air fryer drawer to 204ºC. Place the steak roll-up in the zone 1 air fryer drawer. Air fry for 7 minutes. Flip the steak and cook for an additional 7 minutes, until an instant-read thermometer reads 49ºC for medium-rare (adjust the cooking time for your desired doneness).

Sausage and Pork Meatballs

Prep time: 15 minutes | Cook time: 8 to 12 minutes | Serves 8

1 large egg	1 teaspoon minced garlic
1 teaspoon gelatin	1 teaspoon dried oregano
450 g pork mince	¼ teaspoon red pepper flakes
230 g Italian-seasoned sausage,	Sea salt and freshly ground
casings removed, crumbled	black pepper, to taste
80 ml Parmesan cheese	Keto-friendly marinara sauce,
60 ml finely diced onion	for serving
1 tablespoon tomato paste	

1. Beat the egg in a small bowl and sprinkle with the gelatin. Allow to sit for 5 minutes. 2. In a large bowl, combine the pork mince, sausage, Parmesan, onion, tomato paste, garlic, oregano, and red pepper flakes. Season with salt and black pepper. 3. Stir the gelatin mixture, then add it to the other ingredients and, using clean hands, mix to ensure that everything is well combined. Form into 1½-inch round meatballs. 4. Set the air fryer to 204ºC. Place the meatballs in the two air fryer drawers in a single layer. Air fry for 5 minutes. Flip and cook for 3 to 7 minutes more, or until an instant-read thermometer reads 72ºC.

Mozzarella Stuffed Beef and Pork Meatballs

Prep time: 15 minutes | Cook time: 12 minutes | Serves 4 to 6

1 tablespoon olive oil
1 small onion, finely chopped
1 to 2 cloves garlic, minced
340 g beef mince
340 g pork mince
180 ml bread crumbs
60 ml grated Parmesan cheese

60 ml finely chopped fresh parsley
½ teaspoon dried oregano
1½ teaspoons salt
Freshly ground black pepper, to taste
2 eggs, lightly beaten
140 g low-moisture Mozzarella or other melting cheese, cut into
1-inch cubes

1. Preheat a skillet over medium-high heat. Add the oil and cook the onion and garlic until tender, but not browned. 2. Transfer the onion and garlic to a large bowl and add the beef, pork, bread crumbs, Parmesan cheese, parsley, oregano, salt, pepper and eggs. Mix well until all the ingredients are combined. Divide the mixture into 12 evenly sized balls. Make one meatball at a time, by pressing a hole in the meatball mixture with the finger and pushing a piece of Mozzarella cheese into the hole. Mold the meat back into a ball, enclosing the cheese. 3. Preheat the air fryer to 192°C. 4. Transfer meatballs to the two air fryer drawers and air fry for 12 minutes, shaking the drawers and turning the meatballs twice during the cooking process. Serve warm.

Italian Sausage and Cheese Meatballs

Prep time: 10 minutes | Cook time: 20 minutes | Serves 4

230 g sausage meat with Italian seasoning added to taste
230 g 85% lean beef mince
120 ml shredded sharp Cheddar cheese

½ teaspoon onion granules
½ teaspoon garlic powder
½ teaspoon black pepper

1. In a large bowl, gently mix the sausage meat, beef mince, cheese, onion granules, garlic powder, and pepper until well combined. 2. Form the mixture into 16 meatballs. Place the meatballs in a single layer in the two air fryer drawers. Set the air fryer to 176°C for 20 minutes, turning the meatballs halfway through the cooking time. Use a meat thermometer to ensure the meatballs have reached an internal temperature of 72°C (medium).

Chapter 5 Fish and Seafood

Chapter 5 Fish and Seafood

Country Prawns

Prep time: 10 minutes | Cook time: 15 to 20 minutes | Serves 4

455 g large prawns, peeled and deveined, with tails on
455 g smoked sausage, cut into thick slices
2 corn cobs, quartered
1 courgette, cut into bite-sized pieces
1 red bell pepper, cut into chunks
1 tablespoon Old Bay seasoning
2 tablespoons olive oil
Cooking spray

1. Preheat the air fryer to 204°C. Spray the air fryer drawer lightly with cooking spray. 2. In a large bowl, mix the prawns, sausage, corn, courgette, bell pepper, and Old Bay seasoning, and toss to coat with the spices. Add the olive oil and toss again until evenly coated. 3. Spread the mixture in the two air fryer drawers in a single layer. 4. Air fry for 15 to 20 minutes, or until cooked through, shaking the drawers every 5 minutes for even cooking. 5. Serve immediately.

Prawn Creole Casserole and Garlic Lemon Scallops

Prep time: 25 minutes | Cook time: 25 minutes | Serves 8

Prawn Creole Casserole:
360 g prawns, peeled and deveined
50 g chopped celery
50 g chopped onion
50 g chopped green bell pepper
2 large eggs, beaten
240 ml single cream
1 tablespoon butter, melted
1 tablespoon cornflour
1 teaspoon Creole seasoning
¾ teaspoon salt
½ teaspoon freshly ground black pepper
120 g shredded Cheddar cheese
Cooking spray
Garlic Lemon Scallops:
4 tablespoons salted butter, melted
4 teaspoons peeled and finely minced garlic
½ small lemon, zested and juiced
8 sea scallops, 30 g each, cleaned and patted dry
¼ teaspoon salt
¼ teaspoon ground black pepper

Make the Prawn Creole Casserole (zone 1 drawer): 1. In a medium bowl, stir together the prawns, celery, onion, and green pepper. 2. In another medium bowl, whisk the eggs, single cream, butter, cornflour, Creole seasoning, salt, and pepper until blended. Stir the egg mixture into the prawn mixture. Add the cheese and stir to combine. 3. Preheat the air fryer to 150°C. Spritz a baking pan with oil. 4. Transfer the prawn mixture to the prepared pan and place it in the zone 1 air fryer drawer. 5. Bake for 25 minutes, stirring every 10 minutes, until a knife inserted into the center comes out clean. 6. Serve immediately.
Make the Garlic Lemon Scallops (zone 2 drawer): 1. In a small bowl, mix butter, garlic, lemon zest, and lemon juice. Place scallops in an ungreased round nonstick baking dish. Pour butter mixture over scallops, then sprinkle with salt and pepper. 2. Place dish into the zone 2 air fryer drawer. Adjust the temperature to 182°C and bake for 10 minutes. Scallops will be opaque and firm, and have an internal temperature of 56°C when done. Serve warm.

Rainbow Salmon Kebabs and Tuna Melt

Prep time: 13 minutes | Cook time: 10 minutes | Serves 3

Rainbow Salmon Kebabs:
170 g boneless, skinless salmon, cut into 1-inch cubes
¼ medium red onion, peeled and cut into 1-inch pieces
½ medium yellow bell pepper, seeded and cut into 1-inch pieces
½ medium courgette, trimmed and cut into ½-inch slices
1 tablespoon olive oil
½ teaspoon salt
¼ teaspoon ground black pepper
Tuna Melt:
Olive or vegetable oil, for spraying
140 g can tuna, drained
1 tablespoon mayonnaise
¼ teaspoon garlic granules, plus more for garnish
2 teaspoons unsalted butte
2 slices sandwich bread of choice
2 slices Cheddar cheese

Make the Rainbow Salmon Kebabs (zone 1 drawer): 1. Using one (6-inch) skewer, skewer 1 piece salmon, then 1 piece onion, 1 piece bell pepper, and finally 1 piece courgette. Repeat this pattern with additional skewers to make four kebabs total. Drizzle with olive oil and sprinkle with salt and black pepper. 2. Place kebabs into the ungreased zone 1 air fryer drawer. Adjust the temperature to 204°C and air fry for 8 minutes, turning kebabs halfway through cooking. Salmon will easily flake and have an internal temperature of at least 64°C when done; vegetables will be tender. Serve warm.
Make the Tuna Melt (zone 2 drawer): 1. Line the zone 2 air fryer drawer with baking paper and spray lightly with oil. 2. In a medium bowl, mix together the tuna, mayonnaise, and garlic. 3. Spread 1 teaspoon of butter on each slice of bread and place one slice butter-side down in the prepared drawer. 4. Top with a slice of cheese, the tuna mixture, another slice of cheese, and the other slice of bread, butter-side up. 5. Air fry at 204°C for 5 minutes, flip, and cook for another 5 minutes, until browned and crispy. 6. Sprinkle with additional garlic, before cutting in half and serving.

Coconut Cream Mackerel

Prep time: 10 minutes | Cook time: 6 minutes | Serves 4

900 g mackerel fillet	1 teaspoon cumin seeds
240 ml coconut cream	1 garlic clove, peeled, chopped
1 teaspoon ground coriander	

1. Chop the mackerel roughly and sprinkle it with coconut cream, ground coriander, cumin seeds, and garlic. 2. Then put the fish in the two air fryer drawers and cook at 204°C for 6 minutes.

Scallops and Spinach with Cream Sauce and Confetti Salmon Burgers

Prep time: 15 minutes | Cook time: 12 minutes | Serves 6

Scallops and Spinach with Cream Sauce:	salmon, flaked with a fork
Vegetable oil spray	40 g minced spring onions, white and light green parts only
280 g frozen spinach, thawed and drained	40 g minced red bell pepper
8 jumbo sea scallops	40 g minced celery
Kosher or coarse sea salt, and black pepper, to taste	2 small lemons
180 ml heavy cream	1 teaspoon crab boil seasoning such as Old Bay
1 tablespoon tomato paste	½ teaspoon kosher or coarse sea salt
1 tablespoon chopped fresh basil	½ teaspoon black pepper
1 teaspoon minced garlic	1 egg, beaten
Confetti Salmon Burgers:	30 g fresh bread crumbs
400 g cooked fresh or canned	Vegetable oil, for spraying

Make the Scallops and Spinach with Cream Sauce (zone 1 drawer): 1. Spray a baking pan with vegetable oil spray. Spread the thawed spinach in an even layer in the bottom of the pan. 2. Spray both sides of the scallops with vegetable oil spray. Season lightly with salt and pepper. Arrange the scallops on top of the spinach. 3. In a small bowl, whisk together the cream, tomato paste, basil, garlic, ½ teaspoon salt, and ½ teaspoon pepper. Pour the sauce over the scallops and spinach. 4. Place the pan in the zone 1 air fryer drawer. Set the temperature to 176°C for 10 minutes. Use a meat thermometer to ensure the scallops have an internal temperature of 56°C.
Make the Confetti Salmon Burgers (zone 2 drawer): 1. In a large bowl, combine the salmon, vegetables, the zest and juice of 1 of the lemons, crab boil seasoning, salt, and pepper. Add the egg and bread crumbs and stir to combine. Form the mixture into 4 patties weighing approximately 140 g each. Chill until firm, about 15 minutes. 2. Preheat the 2 air fryer drawer to 204°C. 3. Spray the salmon patties with oil on all sides and spray the zone 2 air fryer drawer to prevent sticking. Air fry for 12 minutes, flipping halfway through, until the burgers are browned and cooked through. Cut the remaining lemon into 4 wedges and serve with the burgers.

Scallops Gratiné with Parmesan

Prep time: 10 minutes | Cook time: 9 minutes | Serves 2

Scallops:	½ teaspoon black pepper
120 ml single cream	455 g sea scallops
45 g grated Parmesan cheese	Topping:
235 g thinly sliced spring onions	30 g panko bread crumbs
5 g chopped fresh parsley	20 g grated Parmesan cheese
3 cloves garlic, minced	Vegetable oil spray
½ teaspoon kosher or coarse sea salt	For Serving:
	Lemon wedges
	Crusty French bread (optional)

1. For the scallops: In a baking pan, combine the single cream, cheese, spring onions, parsley, garlic, salt, and pepper. Stir in the scallops. 2. For the topping: In a small bowl, combine the bread crumbs and cheese. Sprinkle evenly over the scallops. Spray the topping with vegetable oil spray. 3. Place the pan in the zone 1 air fryer drawer. Set the temperature to 164°C for 6 minutes. Set the temperature to 204°C for 3 minutes until the topping has browned. 4. To serve: Squeeze the lemon wedges over the gratin and serve with crusty French bread, if desired.

Nutty Prawns with Amaretto Glaze

Prep time: 30 minutes | Cook time: 10 minutes | Serves 10 to 12

120 g plain flour	oil
½ teaspoon baking powder	185 g sliced almonds
1 teaspoon salt	900 g large prawns (about
2 eggs, beaten	32 to 40 prawns), peeled and
120 ml milk	deveined, tails left on
2 tablespoons olive or vegetable	470 ml amaretto liqueur

1. Combine the flour, baking powder and salt in a large bowl. Add the eggs, milk and oil and stir until it forms a smooth batter. Coarsely crush the sliced almonds into a second shallow dish with your hands. 2. Dry the prawns well with paper towels. Dip the prawns into the batter and shake off any excess batter, leaving just enough to lightly coat the prawns. Transfer the prawns to the dish with the almonds and coat completely. Place the coated prawns on a plate or baking sheet and when all the prawns have been coated, freeze the prawns for an 1 hour, or as long as a week before air frying. 3. Preheat the air fryer to 204°C. 4. Transfer frozen prawns to the two air fryer drawers. Air fry for 6 minutes. Turn the prawns over and air fry for an additional 4 minutes. 5. While the prawns are cooking, bring the Amaretto to a boil in a small saucepan on the stovetop. Lower the heat and simmer until it has reduced and thickened into a glaze, about 10 minutes. 6. Remove the prawns from the air fryer and brush both sides with the warm amaretto glaze. Serve warm.

Orange-Mustard Glazed Salmon

Prep time: 10 minutes | Cook time: 10 minutes | Serves 2

1 tablespoon orange marmalade
¼ teaspoon grated orange zest plus 1 tablespoon juice
2 teaspoons whole-grain mustard

2 (230 g) skin-on salmon fillets, 1½ inches thick
Salt and pepper, to taste
Vegetable oil spray

1. Preheat the zone 1 air fryer drawer to 204ºC. 2. Make foil sling for air fryer drawer by folding 1 long sheet of aluminum foil so it is 4 inches wide. Lay sheet of foil widthwise across drawer, pressing foil into and up sides of drawer. Fold excess foil as needed so that edges of foil are flush with top of drawer. Lightly spray foil and drawer with vegetable oil spray. 3. Combine marmalade, orange zest and juice, and mustard in bowl. Pat salmon dry with paper towels and season with salt and pepper. Brush tops and sides of fillets evenly with glaze. Arrange fillets skin side down on sling in prepared drawer, spaced evenly apart. Air fry salmon until center is still translucent when checked with the tip of a paring knife and registers 52ºC (for medium-rare), 10 to 14 minutes, using sling to rotate fillets halfway through cooking. 4. Using the sling, carefully remove salmon from air fryer. Slide fish spatula along underside of fillets and transfer to individual serving plates, leaving skin behind. Serve.

Chilean Sea Bass with Olive Relish and Snapper with Tomato

Prep time: 30 minutes | Cook time: 15 minutes | Serves 4

Chilean Sea Bass with Olive Relish:
Olive oil spray
2 (170 g) Chilean sea bass fillets or other firm-fleshed white fish
3 tablespoons extra-virgin olive oil
½ teaspoon ground cumin
½ teaspoon kosher or coarse sea salt
½ teaspoon black pepper
60 g pitted green olives, diced
10 g finely diced onion
1 teaspoon chopped capers

Snapper with Tomato:
2 snapper fillets
1 shallot, peeled and sliced
2 garlic cloves, halved
1 bell pepper, sliced
1 small-sized serrano pepper, sliced
1 tomato, sliced
1 tablespoon olive oil
¼ teaspoon freshly ground black pepper
½ teaspoon paprika
Sea salt, to taste
2 bay leaves

Make the Chilean Sea Bass with Olive Relish (zone 1 drawer): 1. Spray the zone 1 air fryer drawer with the olive oil spray. Drizzle the fillets with the olive oil and sprinkle with the cumin, salt, and pepper. Place the fish in the zone 1 air fryer drawer. Set the air fryer to 164ºC for 10 minutes, or until the fish flakes easily with a fork. 2. Meanwhile, in a small bowl, stir together the olives, onion, and capers. 3. Serve the fish topped with the relish.
Make the Snapper with Tomato (zone 2 drawer): 1. Place two

baking paper sheets on a working surface. Place the fish in the center of one side of the baking paper. 2. Top with the shallot, garlic, peppers, and tomato. Drizzle olive oil over the fish and vegetables. Season with black pepper, paprika, and salt. Add the bay leaves. 3. Fold over the other half of the baking paper. Now, fold the paper around the edges tightly and create a half moon shape, sealing the fish inside. 4. Cook in the zone 2 air fryer drawer at 200ºC for 15 minutes. Serve warm.

Italian Baked Cod

Prep time: 5 minutes | Cook time: 12 minutes | Serves 4

4 cod fillets, 170 g each
2 tablespoons salted butter, melted
1 teaspoon Italian seasoning

¼ teaspoon salt
120 ml tomato-based pasta sauce

1. Place cod into an ungreased round nonstick baking dish. Pour butter over cod and sprinkle with Italian seasoning and salt. Top with pasta sauce. 2. Place dish into the two air fryer drawers. Adjust the temperature to 176ºC and bake for 12 minutes. Fillets will be lightly browned, easily flake, and have an internal temperature of at least 64ºC when done. Serve warm.

Fish Cakes

Prep time: 30 minutes | Cook time: 10 to 12 minutes | Serves 4

1 large russet potato, mashed
340 g cod or other white fish
Salt and pepper, to taste
Olive or vegetable oil for misting or cooking spray
1 large egg

50 g potato starch
60 g panko breadcrumbs
1 tablespoon fresh chopped chives
2 tablespoons minced onion

1. Peel potatoes, cut into cubes, and cook on stovetop till soft. 2. Salt and pepper raw fish to taste. Mist with oil or cooking spray, and air fry at 182ºC for 6 to 8 minutes, until fish flakes easily. If fish is crowded, rearrange halfway through cooking to ensure all pieces cook evenly. 3. Transfer fish to a plate and break apart to cool. 4. Beat egg in a shallow dish. 5. Place potato starch in another shallow dish, and panko crumbs in a third dish. 6. When potatoes are done, drain in colander and rinse with cold water. 7. In a large bowl, mash the potatoes and stir in the chives and onion. Add salt and pepper to taste, then stir in the fish. 8. If needed, stir in a tablespoon of the beaten egg to help bind the mixture. 9. Shape into 8 small, fat patties. Dust lightly with potato starch, dip in egg, and roll in panko crumbs. Spray both sides with oil or cooking spray. 10. Air fry for 10 to 12 minutes, until golden brown and crispy.

Thai Prawn Skewers and Lemon-Tarragon Fish en Papillote

Prep time: 25 minutes | Cook time: 15 minutes | Serves 5

Lemon-Tarragon Fish en Papillote:
Salt and pepper, to taste
340 g extra-large prawns, peeled and deveined
1 tablespoon vegetable oil
1 teaspoon honey
½ teaspoon grated lime zest plus 1 tablespoon juice, plus lime wedges for serving
6 (6-inch) wooden skewers
3 tablespoons creamy peanut butter
3 tablespoons hot tap water
1 tablespoon chopped fresh coriander
1 teaspoon fish sauce
Lemon-Tarragon Fish en

Papillote:
2 tablespoons salted butter, melted
1 tablespoon fresh lemon juice
½ teaspoon dried tarragon, crushed, or 2 sprigs fresh tarragon
1 teaspoon kosher or coarse sea salt
85 g julienned carrots
435 g julienned fennel, or 1 stalk julienned celery
75 g thinly sliced red bell pepper
2 cod fillets, 170 g each, thawed if frozen
Vegetable oil spray
½ teaspoon black pepper

Make the Lemon-Tarragon Fish en Papillote (zone 1 drawer): 1. Preheat the air fryer to 204ºC. 2. Dissolve 2 tablespoons salt in 1 litre cold water in a large container. Add prawns, cover, and refrigerate for 15 minutes. 3. Remove prawns from brine and pat dry with paper towels. Whisk oil, honey, lime zest, and ¼ teaspoon pepper together in a large bowl. Add prawns and toss to coat. Thread prawns onto skewers, leaving about ¼ inch between each prawns (3 or 4 prawns per skewer). 4. Arrange 3 skewers in the zone 1 air fryer drawer, parallel to each other and spaced evenly apart. Arrange remaining 3 skewers on top, perpendicular to the bottom layer. Air fry until prawns are opaque throughout, 6 to 8 minutes, flipping and rotating skewers halfway through cooking. 5. Whisk peanut butter, hot tap water, lime juice, coriander, and fish sauce together in a bowl until smooth. Serve skewers with peanut dipping sauce and lime wedges.
Make the Lemon-Tarragon Fish en Papillote (zone 2 drawer): 1. In a medium bowl, combine the butter, lemon juice, tarragon, and ½ teaspoon of the salt. Whisk well until you get a creamy sauce. Add the carrots, fennel, and bell pepper and toss to combine; set aside. 2. Cut two squares of baking paper each large enough to hold one fillet and half the vegetables. Spray the fillets with vegetable oil spray. Season both sides with the remaining ½ teaspoon salt and the black pepper. 3. Lay one fillet down on each baking paper square. Top each with half the vegetables. Pour any remaining sauce over the vegetables. 4. Fold over the baking paper and crimp the sides in small, tight folds to hold the fish, vegetables, and sauce securely inside the packet. Place the packets in the zone 2 air fryer drawer. Set the air fryer to 176ºC for 15 minutes. 5. Transfer each packet to a plate. Cut open with scissors just before serving (be careful, as the steam inside will be hot).

Herbed Prawns Pita

Prep time: 5 minutes | Cook time: 8 minutes | Serves 4

455 g medium prawns, peeled and deveined
2 tablespoons olive oil
1 teaspoon dried oregano
½ teaspoon dried thyme
½ teaspoon garlic powder
¼ teaspoon onion powder
½ teaspoon salt

¼ teaspoon black pepper
4 whole wheat pitas
110 g feta cheese, crumbled
75 g shredded lettuce
1 tomato, diced
45 g black olives, sliced
1 lemon

1. Preheat the oven to 192ºC. 2. In a medium bowl, combine the prawns with the olive oil, oregano, thyme, garlic powder, onion powder, salt, and black pepper. 3. Pour prawns in a single layer in the two air fryer drawers and roast for 6 to 8 minutes, or until cooked through. 4. Remove from the air fryer and divide into warmed pitas with feta, lettuce, tomato, olives, and a squeeze of lemon.

Sweet Tilapia Fillets

Prep time: 5 minutes | Cook time: 14 minutes | Serves 4

2 tablespoons granulated sweetener
1 tablespoon apple cider

vinegar
4 tilapia fillets, boneless
1 teaspoon olive oil

1. Mix apple cider vinegar with olive oil and sweetener. 2. Then rub the tilapia fillets with the sweet mixture and put in the two air fryer drawers in one layer. Cook the fish at 182ºC for 7 minutes per side.

Prawns Curry

Prep time: 30 minutes | Cook time: 10 minutes | Serves 4

180 ml unsweetened full-fat coconut milk
10 g finely chopped yellow onion
2 teaspoons garam masala
1 tablespoon minced fresh ginger
1 tablespoon minced garlic

1 teaspoon ground turmeric
1 teaspoon salt
¼ to ½ teaspoon cayenne pepper
455 g raw prawns (21 to 25 count), peeled and deveined
2 teaspoons chopped fresh coriander

1. In a large bowl, stir together the coconut milk, onion, garam masala, ginger, garlic, turmeric, salt and cayenne, until well blended. 2. Add the prawns and toss until coated with sauce on all sides. Marinate at room temperature for 30 minutes. 3. Transfer the prawns and marinade to a baking pan. Place the pan in the zone 1 air fryer drawer. Set the temperature to 192ºC for 10 minutes, stirring halfway through the cooking time. 4. Transfer the prawns to a serving bowl or platter. Sprinkle with the cilantro and serve.

Steamed Cod with Garlic and Swiss Chard

Prep time: 5 minutes | Cook time: 12 minutes | Serves 4

1 teaspoon salt
½ teaspoon dried oregano
½ teaspoon dried thyme
½ teaspoon garlic powder
4 cod fillets

½ white onion, thinly sliced
135 g Swiss chard, washed, stemmed, and torn into pieces
60 ml olive oil
1 lemon, quartered

1. Preheat the air fryer to 192ºC. 2. In a small bowl, whisk together the salt, oregano, thyme, and garlic powder. 3. Tear off four pieces of aluminum foil, with each sheet being large enough to envelop one cod fillet and a quarter of the vegetables. 4. Place a cod fillet in the middle of each sheet of foil, then sprinkle on all sides with the spice mixture. 5. In each foil packet, place a quarter of the onion slices and 30 g Swiss chard, then drizzle 1 tablespoon olive oil and squeeze ¼ lemon over the contents of each foil packet. 6. Fold and seal the sides of the foil packets and then place them into the two air fryer drawers. Steam for 12 minutes. 7. Remove from the drawers, and carefully open each packet to avoid a steam burn.

Parmesan Mackerel with Coriander and Garlic Butter Prawns Scampi

Prep time: 15 minutes | Cook time: 8 minutes | Serves 6

Parmesan Mackerel with Coriander:

340 g mackerel fillet
60 g Parmesan, grated
1 teaspoon ground coriander
1 tablespoon olive oil
Garlic Butter Prawns Scampi:
Sauce:
60 g unsalted butter
2 tablespoons fish stock or chicken broth
2 cloves garlic, minced

2 tablespoons chopped fresh basil leaves
1 tablespoon lemon juice
1 tablespoon chopped fresh parsley, plus more for garnish
1 teaspoon red pepper flakes
Prawns:
455 g large prawns, peeled and deveined, tails removed
Fresh basil sprigs, for garnish

Make the Parmesan Mackerel with Coriander (zone 1 drawer): 1. Sprinkle the mackerel fillet with olive oil and put it in the zone 1 air fryer drawer. 2. Top the fish with ground coriander and Parmesan. 3. Cook the fish at 200ºC for 7 minutes.
Make the Garlic Butter Prawns Scampi (zone 2 drawer): 1. Preheat the zone 2 air fryer drawer to 176ºC. 2. Put all the ingredients for the sauce in a baking pan and stir to incorporate. 3. Transfer the baking pan to the zone 2 air fryer drawer and air fry for 3 minutes, or until the sauce is heated through. 4. Once done, add the prawns to the baking pan, flipping to coat in the sauce. 5. Return to the air fryer and cook for another 5 minutes, or until the prawns are pink and opaque. Stir the prawns twice during cooking. 6. Serve garnished with the parsley and basil sprigs.

Roasted Halibut Steaks with Parsley

Prep time: 5 minutes | Cook time: 10 minutes | Serves 4

455 g halibut steaks
60 ml vegetable oil
2½ tablespoons Worcester sauce
2 tablespoons honey
2 tablespoons vermouth or white wine vinegar

1 tablespoon freshly squeezed lemon juice
1 tablespoon fresh parsley leaves, coarsely chopped
Salt and pepper, to taste
1 teaspoon dried basil

1. Preheat the air fryer to 200ºC. 2. Put all the ingredients in a large mixing dish and gently stir until the fish is coated evenly. 3. Transfer the fish to the zone 1 air fryer drawer and roast for 10 minutes, flipping the fish halfway through, or until the fish reaches an internal temperature of at least 64ºC on a meat thermometer. 4. Let the fish cool for 5 minutes and serve.

Snapper Scampi

Prep time: 5 minutes | Cook time: 8 to 10 minutes | Serves 4

4 skinless snapper or arctic char fillets, 170 g each
1 tablespoon olive oil
3 tablespoons lemon juice, divided
½ teaspoon dried basil

Pinch salt
Freshly ground black pepper, to taste
2 tablespoons butter
2 cloves garlic, minced

1. Rub the fish fillets with olive oil and 1 tablespoon of the lemon juice. Sprinkle with the basil, salt, and pepper, and place in the two air fryer drawers. 2. Air fry the fish at 192ºC for 7 to 8 minutes or until the fish just flakes when tested with a fork. Remove the fish from the drawers and put on a serving plate. Cover to keep warm. 3. In a baking pan, combine the butter, remaining 2 tablespoons lemon juice, and garlic. Bake in the air fryer for 1 to 2 minutes or until the garlic is sizzling. Pour this mixture over the fish and serve

Salmon with Cauliflower

Prep time: 10 minutes | Cook time: 25 minutes | Serves 4

455 g salmon fillet, diced
100 g cauliflower, shredded
1 tablespoon dried coriander
1 tablespoon coconut oil,

melted
1 teaspoon ground turmeric
60 ml coconut cream

1. Mix salmon with cauliflower, dried cilantro, ground turmeric, coconut cream, and coconut oil. 2. Transfer the salmon mixture into the air fryer and cook the meal at 176ºC for 25 minutes. Stir the meal every 5 minutes to avoid the burning.

Blackened Red Snapper

Prep time: 13 minutes | Cook time: 8 to 10 minutes | Serves 4

1½ teaspoons black pepper	4 red snapper fillet portions,
¼ teaspoon thyme	skin on, 110 g each
¼ teaspoon garlic powder	4 thin slices lemon
⅛ teaspoon cayenne pepper	Cooking spray
1 teaspoon olive oil	

1. Mix the spices and oil together to make a paste. Rub into both sides of the fish. 2. Spray the two air fryer drawers with nonstick cooking spray and lay snapper steaks in drawers, skin-side down. 3. Place a lemon slice on each piece of fish. 4. Roast at 200°C for 8 to 10 minutes. The fish will not flake when done, but it should be white through the center.

Pecan-Crusted Catfish

Prep time: 5 minutes | Cook time: 12 minutes | Serves 4

65 g pecans, finely crushed	4 catfish fillets, 110g each
1 teaspoon fine sea salt	For Garnish (Optional):
¼ teaspoon ground black	Fresh oregano
pepper	Pecan halves

1. Spray the two air fryer drawers with avocado oil. Preheat the air fryer to 192°C. 2. In a large bowl, mix the crushed pecan, salt, and pepper. One at a time, dredge the catfish fillets in the mixture, coating them well. Use your hands to press the pecan meal into the fillets. Spray the fish with avocado oil and place them in the two air fryer drawers. 3. Air fry the coated catfish for 12 minutes, or until it flakes easily and is no longer translucent in the center, flipping halfway through. 4. Garnish with oregano sprigs and pecan halves, if desired. 5. Store leftovers in an airtight container in the fridge for up to 3 days. Reheat in a preheated 176°C air fryer for 4 minutes, or until heated through.

Butter-Wine Baked Salmon

Prep time: 5 minutes | Cook time: 10 minutes | Serves 4

4 tablespoons butter, melted	1 tablespoon lime juice
2 cloves garlic, minced	1 teaspoon smoked paprika
Sea salt and ground black	½ teaspoon onion powder
pepper, to taste	4 salmon steaks
60 ml dry white wine or apple	Cooking spray
cider vinegar	

1. Place all the ingredients except the salmon and oil in a shallow dish and stir to mix well. 2. Add the salmon steaks, turning to coat well on both sides. Transfer the salmon to the refrigerator to marinate for 30 minutes. 3. Preheat the air fryer to 182°C. 4. Place the salmon steaks in the two air fryer drawers, discarding any excess marinade. Spray the salmon steaks with cooking spray. 5. Air fry for about 10 minutes, flipping the salmon steaks halfway through, or until cooked to your preferred doneness. 6. Divide the salmon steaks among four plates and serve.

Oyster Po'Boy

Prep time: 20 minutes | Cook time: 5 minutes | Serves 4

105 g plain flour	1 (12-inch) French baguette,
40 g yellow cornmeal	quartered and sliced
1 tablespoon Cajun seasoning	horizontally
1 teaspoon salt	Tartar Sauce, as needed
2 large eggs, beaten	150 g shredded lettuce, divided
1 teaspoon hot sauce	2 tomatoes, cut into slices
455 g pre-shucked oysters	Cooking spray

1. In a shallow bowl, whisk the flour, cornmeal, Cajun seasoning, and salt until blended. In a second shallow bowl, whisk together the eggs and hot sauce. 2. One at a time, dip the oysters in the cornmeal mixture, the eggs, and again in the cornmeal, coating thoroughly. 3. Preheat the zone 1 air fryer drawer to 204°C. Line the zone 1 air fryer drawer with baking paper. 4. Place the oysters on the baking paper and spritz with oil. 5. Air fry for 2 minutes. Shake the drawer, spritz the oysters with oil, and air fry for 3 minutes more until lightly browned and crispy. 6. Spread each sandwich half with Tartar Sauce. Assemble the po'boys by layering each sandwich with fried oysters, ½ cup shredded lettuce, and 2 tomato slices. 7. Serve immediately.

Fish Fillets with Lemon-Dill Sauce

Prep time: 5 minutes | Cook time: 7 minutes | Serves 4

455 g snapper, grouper, or	60 g mayonnaise
salmon fillets	2 tablespoons fresh dill,
Sea salt and freshly ground	chopped, plus more for garnish
black pepper, to taste	1 tablespoon freshly squeezed
1 tablespoon avocado oil	lemon juice
60 g sour cream	½ teaspoon grated lemon zest

1. Pat the fish dry with paper towels and season well with salt and pepper. Brush with the avocado oil. 2. Set the air fryer to 204°C. Place the fillets in the two air fryer drawers and air fry for 1 minute. 3. Lower the air fryer temperature to 164°C and continue cooking for 5 minutes. Flip the fish and cook for 1 minute more or until an instant-read thermometer reads 64°C. (If using salmon, cook it to 52°C for medium-rare.) 4. While the fish is cooking, make the sauce by combining the sour cream, mayonnaise, dill, lemon juice, and lemon zest in a medium bowl. Season with salt and pepper and stir until combined. Refrigerate until ready to serve. 5. Serve the fish with the sauce, garnished with the remaining dill.

Cod with Jalapeño

Prep time: 5 minutes | Cook time: 14 minutes | Serves 4

4 cod fillets, boneless	1 tablespoon avocado oil
1 jalapeño, minced	½ teaspoon minced garlic

1. In the shallow bowl, mix minced jalapeño, avocado oil, and minced garlic. 2. Put the cod fillets in the two air fryer drawers in one layer and top with minced jalapeño mixture. 3. Cook the fish at 185ºC for 7 minutes per side.

Lemony Prawns and Courgette

Prep time: 15 minutes | Cook time: 7 to 8 minutes | Serves 4

570 g extra-large raw prawns, peeled and deveined	1½ teaspoons dried oregano
2 medium courgettes (about 230 g each), halved lengthwise and cut into ½-inch-thick slices	⅛ teaspoon crushed red pepper flakes (optional)
1½ tablespoons olive oil	Juice of ½ lemon
½ teaspoon garlic salt	1 tablespoon chopped fresh mint
	1 tablespoon chopped fresh dill

1. Preheat the air fryer to 176ºC. 2. In a large bowl, combine the prawns, courgette, oil, garlic salt, oregano, and pepper flakes (if using) and toss to coat. 3. Arrange a single layer of the prawns and courgette in the two air fryer drawers. Air fry for 7 to 8 minutes, shaking the drawer halfway, until the courgette is golden and the prawns are cooked through. 4. Transfer to a serving dish and tent with foil while you air fry the remaining prawns and courgette. 5. Top with the lemon juice, mint, and dill and serve.

Classic Fish Sticks with Tartar Sauce

Prep time: 10 minutes | Cook time: 12 to 15 minutes | Serves 4

680 g cod fillets, cut into 1-inch strips	120 ml sour cream
1 teaspoon salt	120 ml mayonnaise
½ teaspoon freshly ground black pepper	3 tablespoons chopped dill pickle
2 eggs	2 tablespoons capers, drained and chopped
70 g almond flour	½ teaspoon dried dill
20 g grated Parmesan cheese	1 tablespoon dill pickle liquid
Tartar Sauce:	(optional)

1. Preheat the air fryer to 204ºC. 2. Season the cod with the salt and black pepper; set aside. 3. In a shallow bowl, lightly beat the eggs. In a second shallow bowl, combine the almond flour and Parmesan cheese. Stir until thoroughly combined. 4. Working with a few pieces at a time, dip the fish into the egg mixture followed by the flour mixture. Press lightly to ensure an even coating. 5. Arrange the fish in a single layer in the two air fryer drawers and spray lightly with olive oil. Pausing halfway through the cooking time to turn the fish, air fry for 12 to 15 minutes, until the fish flakes easily with a fork. Let sit in the drawer for a few minutes before serving with the tartar sauce. 6. To make the tartar sauce: In a small bowl, combine the sour cream, mayonnaise, pickle, capers, and dill. If you prefer a thinner sauce, stir in the pickle liquid.

Cod with Avocado and Garlic Prawns

Prep time: 45 minutes | Cook time: 10 minutes | Serves 5

Cod with Avocado:	Olive or vegetable oil, for spraying
90 g shredded cabbage	
60 ml full-fat sour cream	450 g medium raw prawns, peeled and deveined
2 tablespoons full-fat mayonnaise	6 tablespoons unsalted butter, melted
20 g chopped pickled jalapeños	
2 (85 g) cod fillets	120 g panko bread crumbs
1 teaspoon chilli powder	2 tablespoons garlic granules
1 teaspoon cumin	1 teaspoon salt
½ teaspoon paprika	½ teaspoon freshly ground black pepper
¼ teaspoon garlic powder	
1 medium avocado, peeled, pitted, and sliced	Garlic Butter Sauce:
	115 g unsalted butter
½ medium lime	2 teaspoons garlic granules
Garlic Prawns:	¾ teaspoon salt (omit if using
Prawns:	salted butter)

Make the Cod with Avocado (zone 1 drawer): 1. In a large bowl, place cabbage, sour cream, mayonnaise, and jalapeños. Mix until fully coated. Let sit for 20 minutes in the refrigerator. 2. Sprinkle cod fillets with chilli powder, cumin, paprika, and garlic powder. Place each fillet into the zone 1 air fryer drawer. 3. Adjust the temperature to 188ºC and set the timer for 10 minutes. 4. Flip the fillets halfway through the cooking time. When fully cooked, fish should have an internal temperature of at least 64ºC. 5. To serve, divide slaw mixture into two serving bowls, break cod fillets into pieces and spread over the bowls, and top with avocado. Squeeze lime juice over each bowl. Serve immediately.

Make the Garlic Prawns (zone 2 drawer): Make the Prawns 1. Preheat the air fryer to 204ºC. Line the zone 2 air fryer drawer with baking paper and spray lightly with oil. 2. Place the prawns and melted butter in a zip-top plastic bag, seal, and shake well, until evenly coated. 3. In a medium bowl, mix together the breadcrumbs, garlic, salt, and black pepper. 4. Add the prawns to the panko mixture and toss until evenly coated. Shake off any excess coating. 5. Place the prawns in the prepared drawer and spray lightly with oil. 6. Cook for 8 to 10 minutes, flipping and spraying with oil after 4 to 5 minutes, until golden brown and crispy. Make the Garlic Butter Sauce 7. In a microwave-safe bowl, combine the butter, garlic, and salt and microwave on 50% power for 30 to 60 seconds, stirring every 15 seconds, until completely melted. 8. Serve the prawns immediately with the garlic butter sauce on the side for dipping.

Chapter 6 Fast and Easy Everyday Favourites

Chapter 6 Fast and Easy Everyday Favourites

Cheesy Potato Patties

Prep time: 5 minutes | Cook time: 10 minutes | Serves 8

900 g white potatoes
120 ml finely chopped spring onions
½ teaspoon freshly ground black pepper, or more to taste
1 tablespoon fine sea salt

½ teaspoon hot paprika
475 ml shredded Colby or Monterey Jack cheese
60 ml rapeseed oil
235 ml crushed crackers

1.Preheat the air fryer to 182°C. Boil the potatoes until soft. Dry them off and peel them before mashing thoroughly, leaving no lumps. 2. Combine the mashed potatoes with spring onions, pepper, salt, paprika, and cheese. Mould the mixture into balls with your hands and press with your palm to flatten them into patties. 3. In a shallow dish, combine the rapeseed oil and crushed crackers. Coat the patties in the crumb mixture. 4. Bake the patties for about 10 minutes, in the two drawers. Serve hot.

Traditional Queso Fundido and Air Fried Shishito Peppers

Prep time: 15 minutes | Cook time: 25 minutes | Serves 7

Traditional Queso Fundido:
110 g fresh Mexican (or Spanish if unavailable) chorizo, casings removed
1 medium onion, chopped
3 cloves garlic, minced
235 ml chopped tomato
2 jalapeños, deseeded and diced
2 teaspoons ground cumin
475 ml shredded Oaxaca or Mozzarella cheese
120 ml half-and-half (60 ml

whole milk and 60 ml cream combined)
Celery sticks or tortilla chips, for serving
Air Fried Shishito Peppers:
230 g shishito or Padron peppers (about 24)
1 tablespoon olive oil
Coarse sea salt, to taste
Lemon wedges, for serving
Cooking spray

Make the Traditional Queso Fundido (zone 1 drawer): 1. Preheat the air fryer to 204°C. 2. In a baking pan, combine the chorizo, onion, garlic, tomato, jalapeños, and cumin. Stir to combine. 3. Place the pan in the zone 1 air fryer drawer. Air fry for 15 minutes, or until the sausage is cooked, stirring halfway through the cooking time to break up the sausage. 4. Add the cheese and half-and-half;

stir to combine. Air fry for 10 minutes, or until the cheese has melted. 5. Serve with celery sticks or tortilla chips.
Make the Air Fried Shishito Peppers (zone 2 drawer): 1. Preheat the air fryer to 204°C. 2. Spritz the zone 2 air fryer drawer with cooking spray. Toss the peppers with olive oil in a large bowl to coat well. 3. Arrange the peppers in the preheated air fryer. Air fryer for 5 minutes or until blistered and lightly charred. Shake the drawer and sprinkle the peppers with salt halfway through the cooking time. 4. Transfer the peppers onto a plate and squeeze the lemon wedges on top before serving.

Beetroot Salad with Lemon Vinaigrette and Easy Roasted Asparagus

Prep time: 15 minutes | Cook time: 12 to 15 minutes | Serves 8

Beetroot Salad with Lemon Vinaigrette:
6 medium red and golden beetroots, peeled and sliced
1 teaspoon olive oil
¼ teaspoon rock salt
120 ml crumbled feta cheese
2 L mixed greens
Cooking spray
Vinaigrette:

2 teaspoons olive oil
2 tablespoons chopped fresh chives
Juice of 1 lemon
Easy Roasted Asparagus:
450 g asparagus, trimmed and halved crosswise
1 teaspoon extra-virgin olive oil
Salt and pepper, to taste
Lemon wedges, for serving

Make the Beetroot Salad with Lemon Vinaigrette (zone 1 drawer): 1. Preheat the air fryer to 182°C. In a large bowl, toss the beetroots, olive oil, and rock salt. 2. Spray the zone 1 air fryer drawer with cooking spray, then place the beetroots in the drawer and air fry for 12 to 15 minutes or until tender. 3. While the beetroots cook, make the vinaigrette in a large bowl by whisking together the olive oil, lemon juice, and chives. Remove the beetroots from the air fryer, toss in the vinaigrette, and allow to cool for 5 minutes. 4. Add the feta and serve on top of the mixed greens.
Make the Easy Roasted Asparagus (zone 2 drawer): 1. Preheat the air fryer to 204°C. Toss the asparagus with the oil, ⅛ teaspoon salt, and ⅛ teaspoon pepper in bowl. 2. Transfer to zone 2 air fryer drawer. Place the drawer in air fryer and roast for 6 to 8 minutes, or until tender and bright green, tossing halfway through cooking. 3. Season with salt and pepper and serve with lemon wedges.

Corn Fritters

235 ml self-raising flour	60 ml buttermilk
1 tablespoon sugar	180 ml corn kernels
1 teaspoon salt	60 ml minced onion
1 large egg, lightly beaten	Cooking spray

1.Preheat the zone 1 air fryer drawer to 176°C. 2. Line the zone 1 air fryer drawer with parchment paper. 3. In a medium bowl, whisk the flour, sugar, and salt until blended. Stir in the egg and buttermilk. Add the corn and minced onion. Mix well. Shape the corn fritter batter into 12 balls. 4. Place the fritters on the parchment and spritz with oil. Bake for 4 minutes. Flip the fritters, spritz them with oil, and bake for 4 minutes more until firm and lightly browned. 5. Serve immediately.

Crunchy Fried Okra and Herb-Roasted Veggies

Crunchy Fried Okra:	Herb-Roasted Veggies:
235 ml self-raising yellow cornmeal	1 red pepper, sliced
1 teaspoon Italian-style seasoning	1 (230 g) package sliced mushrooms
1 teaspoon paprika	235 ml green beans, cut into 2-inch pieces
1 teaspoon salt	80 ml diced red onion
½ teaspoon freshly ground black pepper	3 garlic cloves, sliced
2 large eggs, beaten	1 teaspoon olive oil
475 ml okra slices	½ teaspoon dried basil
Cooking spray	½ teaspoon dried tarragon

Make the Crunchy Fried Okra (zone 1 drawer): 1. Preheat the air fryer to 204°C. 2. Line the zone 1 air fryer drawer with parchment paper. 3. In a shallow bowl, whisk the cornmeal, Italian-style seasoning, paprika, salt, and pepper until blended. Place the beaten eggs in a second shallow bowl. Add the okra to the beaten egg and stir to coat. Add the egg and okra mixture to the cornmeal mixture and stir until coated. 4. Place the okra on the parchment and spritz it with oil. Air fry for 4 minutes. Shake the zone 1 drawer, spritz the okra with oil, and air fry for 4 to 6 minutes more until lightly browned and crispy. 5. Serve immediately.

Make the Herb-Roasted Veggies (zone 2 drawer): 1. Preheat the air fryer to 176°C. 2. In a medium bowl, mix the red pepper, mushrooms, green beans, red onion, and garlic. Drizzle with the olive oil. Toss to coat. Add the herbs and toss again. 3. Place the vegetables in the zone 2 air fryer drawer. Roast for 14 to 18 minutes, or until tender. 4. Serve immediately.

Cheesy Chilli Toast and Cheesy Baked Grits

Cheesy Chilli Toast:	Cheesy Baked Grits:
2 tablespoons grated Parmesan cheese	180 ml hot water
2 tablespoons grated Mozzarella cheese	2 (28 g) packages instant grits
2 teaspoons salted butter, at room temperature	1 large egg, beaten
10 to 15 thin slices serrano chilli or jalapeño	1 tablespoon butter, melted
2 slices sourdough bread	2 cloves garlic, minced
½ teaspoon black pepper	½ to 1 teaspoon red pepper flakes
	235 ml shredded Cheddar cheese or jalapeño Jack cheese

Make the Cheesy Chilli Toast (zone 1 drawer): 1. Preheat the air fryer to 164°C. 2. In a small bowl, stir together the Parmesan, Mozzarella, butter, and chillies. Spread half the mixture onto one side of each slice of bread. Sprinkle with the pepper. 3. Place the slices, cheese-side up, in the zone 1 air fryer drawer. Bake for 5 minutes, or until the cheese has melted and started to brown slightly. 4. Serve immediately.

Make the Cheesy Baked Grits (zone 2 drawer): 1. Preheat the air fryer to 204°C. 2. In a baking pan, combine the water, grits, egg, butter, garlic, and red pepper flakes. Stir until well combined. Stir in the shredded cheese. 3. Place the pan in the zone 2 air fryer drawer and air fry for 12 minutes, or until the grits have cooked through and a knife inserted near the centre comes out clean. 4. Let stand for 5 minutes before serving.

Purple Potato Chips with Rosemary

235 ml Greek yoghurt	miniature potatoes
2 chipotle chillies, minced	1 teaspoon olive oil
2 tablespoons adobo or chipotle sauce	2 teaspoons minced fresh rosemary leaves
1 teaspoon paprika	⅛ teaspoon cayenne pepper
1 tablespoon lemon juice	¼ teaspoon coarse sea salt
10 purple fingerling or	

1.Preheat the air fryer to 204°C. 2. In a medium bowl, combine the yoghurt, minced chillies, adobo sauce, paprika, and lemon juice. Mix well and refrigerate. 3. Wash the potatoes and dry them with paper towels. Slice the potatoes lengthwise, as thinly as possible. You can use a mandoline, a vegetable peeler, or a very sharp knife. Combine the potato slices in a medium bowl and drizzle with the olive oil; toss to coat. 4. Air fry the chips in the two air fryer drawers, for 9 to 14 minutes. Use tongs to gently rearrange the chips halfway during cooking time. Sprinkle the chips with the rosemary, cayenne pepper, and sea salt. 5. Serve with the chipotle sauce for dipping.

Rosemary and Orange Roasted Chickpeas

Prep time: 5 minutes | Cook time: 10 to 12 minutes |
Makes 1 L

1 L cooked chickpeas	1 teaspoon paprika
2 tablespoons vegetable oil	Zest of 1 orange
1 teaspoon rock salt	1 tablespoon chopped fresh
1 teaspoon cumin	rosemary

1.Preheat the air fryer to 204°C. Make sure the chickpeas are completely dry prior to roasting. 2. In a medium bowl, toss the chickpeas with oil, salt, cumin, and paprika. 3. Spread the chickpeas in a single layer in the two air fryer drawers. Air fry for 10 to 12 minutes until crisp, shaking once halfway through. 4. Return the warm chickpeas to the bowl and toss with the orange zest and rosemary. 5. Allow to cool completely. Serve.

Peppery Brown Rice Fritters

Prep time: 10 minutes | Cook time: 8 to 10 minutes |
Serves 4

1 (284 g) bag frozen cooked brown rice, thawed	2 tablespoons minced fresh basil
1 egg	3 tablespoons grated Parmesan cheese
3 tablespoons brown rice flour	
80 ml finely grated carrots	2 teaspoons olive oil
80 ml minced red pepper	

1.Preheat the air fryer to 192°C. 2. In a small bowl, combine the thawed rice, egg, and flour and mix to blend. Stir in the carrots, pepper, basil, and Parmesan cheese. 3. Form the mixture into 8 fritters and drizzle with the olive oil. Put the fritters carefully into the two air fryer drawers. Air fry for 8 to 10 minutes, or until the fritters are golden brown and cooked through. 4. Serve immediately.

Beery and Crunchy Onion Rings

Prep time: 10 minutes | Cook time: 16 minutes |
Serves 2 to 4

160 ml plain flour	180 ml beer
1 teaspoon paprika	350 ml breadcrumbs
½ teaspoon bicarbonate of soda	1 tablespoons olive oil
1 teaspoon salt	1 large Vidalia or sweet onion, peeled and sliced into ½-inch rings
½ teaspoon freshly ground black pepper	
1 egg, beaten	Cooking spray

1.Preheat the air fryer to 182°C. 2. Spritz the two air fryer drawers with cooking spray. Combine the flour, paprika, bicarbonate of soda, salt, and ground black pepper in a bowl. Stir to mix well. 3. Combine the egg and beer in a separate bowl. Stir to mix well. 4. Make a well in the centre of the flour mixture, then pour the egg mixture in the well. Stir to mix everything well. Pour the breadcrumbs and olive oil in a shallow plate. Stir to mix well. 5. Dredge the onion rings gently into the flour and egg mixture, then shake the excess off and put into the plate of breadcrumbs. Flip to coat both sides well. 6. Arrange the onion rings in the preheated air fryer drawers. Air fry for 16 minutes or until golden brown and crunchy. Flip the rings and put the bottom rings to the top halfway through. 7. Serve immediately.

Air Fried Broccoli

Prep time: 5 minutes | Cook time: 6 minutes | Serves 3

4 egg yolks	Salt and pepper, to taste
60 ml butter, melted	475 ml broccoli florets
475 ml coconut flour	

1.Preheat the air fryer to 204°C. 2. In a bowl, whisk the egg yolks and melted butter together. 3. Throw in the coconut flour, salt and pepper, then stir again to combine well. 4. Dip each broccoli floret into the mixture and place in the two air fryer drawers. Take care when removing them from the air fryer and serve immediately.

Spinach and Carrot Balls and Simple Pea Delight

Prep time: 15 minutes | Cook time: 15 minutes |
Serves 6-8

Spinach and Carrot Balls:	flakes
2 slices toasted bread	1 tablespoon flour
1 carrot, peeled and grated	Simple Pea Delight :
1 package fresh spinach, blanched and chopped	235 ml flour
	1 teaspoon baking powder
½ onion, chopped	3 eggs
1 egg, beaten	235 ml coconut milk
½ teaspoon garlic powder	235 ml soft white cheese
1 teaspoon minced garlic	3 tablespoons pea protein
1 teaspoon salt	120 ml chicken or turkey strips
½ teaspoon black pepper	Pinch of sea salt
1 tablespoon Engevita yeast	235 ml Mozzarella cheese

Make the Spinach and Carrot Balls (zone 1 drawer): 1. Preheat the air fryer to 200°C. In a food processor, pulse the toasted bread to form breadcrumbs. 2. Transfer into a shallow dish or bowl. In a bowl, mix together all the other ingredients. Use your hands to shape the mixture into small-sized balls. 3. Roll the balls in the breadcrumbs, ensuring to cover them well. Put in the zone 1 air fryer drawer and air fry for 10 minutes. 4. Serve immediately.

Make the Simple Pea Delight (zone 2 drawer): 1. Preheat the air fryer to 200°C. 2. In a large bowl, mix all ingredients together using a large wooden spoon. 3. Spoon equal amounts of the mixture into muffin cups and bake in the zone 2 drawer for 15 minutes. 4. Serve immediately.

Baked Cheese Sandwich and Bacon Pinwheels

Prep time: 15 minutes | Cook time: 10 minutes | Serves 8

Baked Cheese Sandwich:
2 tablespoons mayonnaise
4 thick slices sourdough bread
4 thick slices Brie cheese
8 slices hot capicola or
prosciutto
Bacon Pinwheels:

1 sheet puff pastry
2 tablespoons maple syrup
60 ml brown sugar
8 slices bacon
Ground black pepper, to taste
Cooking spray

Make the Baked Cheese Sandwich (zone 1 drawer): 1. Preheat the air fryer to 176°C. 2. Spread the mayonnaise on one side of each slice of bread. 3. Place 2 slices of bread in the zone 1 air fryer drawer, mayonnaise-side down. Place the slices of Brie and capicola on the bread and cover with the remaining two slices of bread, mayonnaise-side up. 4. Bake for 8 minutes, or until the cheese has melted. Serve immediately.

Make the Bacon Pinwheels (zone 2 drawer): 1. Preheat the air fryer to 182°C. 2. Spritz the zone 2 air fryer drawer with cooking spray. 3. Roll the puff pastry into a 10-inch square with a rolling pin on a clean work surface, then cut the pastry into 8 strips. 4. Brush the strips with maple syrup and sprinkle with sugar, leaving a 1-inch far end uncovered. 5. Arrange each slice of bacon on each strip, leaving a ⅛-inch length of bacon hang over the end close to you. 6. Sprinkle with black pepper. From the end close to you, roll the strips into pinwheels, then dab the uncovered end with water and seal the rolls. 7. Arrange the pinwheels in the preheated air fryer drawer and spritz with cooking spray. Air fry for 10 minutes or until golden brown. Flip the pinwheels halfway through. 8. Serve immediately.

Air Fried Courgette Sticks

Prep time: 5 minutes | Cook time: 20 minutes | Serves 4

1 medium courgette, cut into 48
sticks
60 ml seasoned breadcrumbs

1 tablespoon melted margarine
Cooking spray

1.Preheat the air fryer to 182°C. 2. Spritz the two air fryer drawers with cooking spray and set aside. 3. In 2 different shallow bowls, add the seasoned breadcrumbs and the margarine. One by one, dredge the courgette sticks into the margarine, then roll in the breadcrumbs to coat evenly. Arrange the crusted sticks on a plate. 4. Place the courgette sticks in the two prepared air fryer drawers. Air fry for 10 minutes, or until golden brown and crispy. Shake the drawers halfway through to cook evenly. 5. When the cooking time is over, transfer the fries to a wire rack. Rest for 5 minutes and serve warm.

Buttery Sweet Potatoes and Beef Bratwursts

Prep time: 10 minutes | Cook time: 15 minutes | Serves 7

Buttery Sweet Potatoes:
2 tablespoons butter, melted
1 tablespoon light brown sugar
2 sweet potatoes, peeled and cut

into ½-inch cubes
Cooking spray
Beef Bratwursts :
4 (85 g) beef bratwursts

Make the Buttery Sweet Potatoes (zone 1 drawer): 1. Preheat the air fryer to 200°C. 2. Line the zone 1 air fryer drawer with parchment paper. 3. In a medium bowl, stir together the melted butter and brown sugar until blended. Toss the sweet potatoes in the butter mixture until coated. 4. Place the sweet potatoes on the parchment and spritz with oil. Air fry for 5 minutes. Shake the drawer, spritz the sweet potatoes with oil, and air fry for 5 minutes more until they're soft enough to cut with a fork. 5. Serve immediately.

Make the Beef Bratwursts (zone 2 drawer): 1. Preheat the air fryer to 200°C. 2. Place the beef bratwursts in the zone 2 air fryer drawer and air fry for 15 minutes, turning once halfway through. 3. Serve hot.

Air Fried Butternut Squash with Chopped Hazelnuts

Prep time: 10 minutes | Cook time: 20 minutes | Makes 700 ml

2 tablespoons whole hazelnuts
700 ml butternut squash,
peeled, deseeded, and cubed
¼ teaspoon rock salt

¼ teaspoon freshly ground
black pepper
2 teaspoons olive oil
Cooking spray

1.Preheat the air fryer to 152°C. 2. Spritz the zone 1 air fryer drawer with cooking spray. 3. Arrange the hazelnuts in the preheated air fryer. Air fry for 3 minutes or until soft. 4. Chopped the hazelnuts roughly and transfer to a small bowl. Set aside. Set the air fryer temperature to 182°C. Spritz with cooking spray. Put the butternut squash in a large bowl, then sprinkle with salt and pepper and drizzle with olive oil. Toss to coat well. 5. Transfer the squash in the zone 1 air fryer drawer. Air fry for 20 minutes or until the squash is soft. Shake the drawer halfway through the frying time. 6. When the frying is complete, transfer the squash onto a plate and sprinkle with chopped hazelnuts before serving.

Easy Devils on Horseback

Prep time: 5 minutes | Cook time: 7 minutes | Serves 12

24 small pitted prunes (128 g)
60 ml crumbled blue cheese, divided

8 slices centre-cut bacon, cut crosswise into thirds

1.Preheat the air fryer to 204ºC. 2. Halve the prunes lengthwise, but don't cut them all the way through. 3. Place ½ teaspoon of cheese in the centre of each prune. 4. Wrap a piece of bacon around each prune and secure the bacon with a toothpick. 5. Arrange a single layer of the prunes in the two air fryer drawers. Air fry for about 7 minutes, flipping halfway, until the bacon is cooked through and crisp. 6. Let cool slightly and serve warm.

Indian-Style Sweet Potato Fries

Prep time: 5 minutes | Cook time: 8 minutes | Makes 20 fries

Seasoning Mixture:
¾ teaspoon ground coriander
½ teaspoon garam masala
½ teaspoon garlic powder
½ teaspoon ground cumin

¼ teaspoon ground cayenne pepper
Fries:
2 large sweet potatoes, peeled
2 teaspoons olive oil

1.Preheat the air fryer to 204ºC. 2. In a small bowl, combine the coriander, garam masala, garlic powder, cumin, and cayenne pepper. Slice the sweet potatoes into ¼-inch-thick fries. 3. In a large bowl, toss the sliced sweet potatoes with the olive oil and the seasoning mixture. 4. Transfer the seasoned sweet potatoes to the two air fryer drawers and fry for 8 minutes, until crispy. 5. Serve warm.

Chapter 7 Holiday Specials

Chapter 7 Holiday Specials

Golden Nuggets

Prep time: 15 minutes | Cook time: 4 minutes |
Makes 20 nuggets

235 ml plain flour, plus more for dusting
1 teaspoon baking powder
½ teaspoon butter, at room temperature, plus more for brushing
¼ teaspoon salt
60 ml water
⅛ teaspoon onion powder
¼ teaspoon garlic powder
⅛ teaspoon seasoning salt
Cooking spray

1.Preheat the air fryer to 188°C. Line the two air fryer drawers with parchment paper. 2. Mix the flour, baking powder, butter, and salt in a large bowl. Stir to mix well. Gradually whisk in the water until a sanity dough forms. Put the dough on a lightly floured work surface, then roll it out into a ½-inch thick rectangle with a rolling pin. 3. Cut the dough into about twenty 1- or 2-inch squares, then arrange the squares in a single layer in the preheated air fryer. 4. Spritz with cooking spray. Combine onion powder, garlic powder, and seasoning salt in a small bowl. Stir to mix well, then sprinkle the squares with the powder mixture. 5. Air fry the dough squares for 4 minutes or until golden brown. Flip the squares halfway through the cooking time. 6. Remove the golden nuggets from the air fryer and brush with more butter immediately. Serve warm.

Simple Air Fried Crispy Brussels Sprouts

Prep time: 5 minutes | Cook time: 20 minutes | Serves 4

¼ teaspoon salt
⅛ teaspoon ground black pepper
1 tablespoon extra-virgin olive
oil
450 g Brussels sprouts, trimmed and halved
Lemon wedges, for garnish

1.Preheat the zone 1 air fryer drawer to 176°C. Combine the salt, black pepper, and olive oil in a large bowl. Stir to mix well. 2. Add the Brussels sprouts to the bowl of mixture and toss to coat well. 3. Arrange the Brussels sprouts in the preheated air fryer. Air fry for 20 minutes or until lightly browned and wilted. Shake the drawer two times during the air frying. 4. Transfer the cooked Brussels sprouts to a large plate and squeeze the lemon wedges on top to serve.

Teriyaki Shrimp Skewers

Prep time: 10 minutes | Cook time: 6 minutes |
Makes 12 skewered shrimp

1½ tablespoons mirin
1½ teaspoons ginger paste
1½ tablespoons soy sauce
12 large shrimp, peeled and
deveined
1 large egg
180 ml panko breadcrumbs
Cooking spray

1.Combine the mirin, ginger paste, and soy sauce in a large bowl. Stir to mix well. Dunk the shrimp in the bowl of mirin mixture, then wrap the bowl in plastic and refrigerate for 1 hour to marinate. 2. Preheat the air fryer to 204°C. Spritz the two air fryer drawers with cooking spray. Run twelve 4-inch skewers through each shrimp. 3. Whisk the egg in the bowl of marinade to combine well. Pour the breadcrumbs on a plate. 4. Dredge the shrimp skewers in the egg mixture, then shake the excess off and roll over the breadcrumbs to coat well. 5. Arrange the shrimp skewers in the preheated air fryer and spritz with cooking spray. Air fry for 6 minutes or until the shrimp are opaque and firm. Flip the shrimp skewers halfway through. 6. Serve immediately.

Southwest Corn and Pepper Roast

Prep time: 10 minutes | Cook time: 10 minutes | Serves 4

For the Corn:
350 ml thawed frozen corn kernels
235 ml mixed diced peppers
1 jalapeño, diced
235 ml diced brown onion
½ teaspoon ancho chilli powder
1 tablespoon fresh lemon juice
1 teaspoon ground cumin
½ teaspoon rock salt
Cooking spray
For Serving:
60 ml feta cheese
60 ml chopped fresh coriander
1 tablespoon fresh lemon juice

1.Preheat the air fryer to 192°C. Spritz the air fryer with cooking spray. 2. Combine the ingredients for the corn in a large bowl. Stir to mix well. 3. Pour the mixture into the zone 1 air fryer drawer. Air fry for 10 minutes or until the corn and peppers are soft. Shake the drawer halfway through the cooking time. 4. Transfer them onto a large plate, then spread with feta cheese and coriander. 5. Drizzle with lemon juice and serve.

Lush Snack Mix

120 ml honey	475 ml granola
3 tablespoons butter, melted	235 ml cashews
1 teaspoon salt	475 ml crispy corn puff cereal
475 ml sesame sticks	475 ml mini pretzel crisps
475 ml pumpkin seeds	

1.In a bowl, combine the honey, butter, and salt. 2. In another bowl, mix the sesame sticks, pumpkin seeds, granola, cashews, corn puff cereal, and pretzel crisps. Combine the contents of the two bowls. 3. Preheat the air fryer to 188℃. Put the mixture in the two air fryer drawers and air fry for 10 to 12 minutes to toast the snack mixture, shaking the drawers frequently. 4. Put the snack mix on a cookie sheet and allow it to cool fully. 5. Serve immediately.

Jewish Blintzes

2 (213 g) packages farmer or ricotta cheese, mashed	60 ml granulated white sugar
60 ml soft white cheese	8 egg roll wrappers
¼ teaspoon vanilla extract	4 tablespoons butter, melted

1.Preheat the air fryer to 192℃. Combine the cheese, soft white cheese, vanilla extract, and sugar in a bowl. Stir to mix well. 2. Unfold the egg roll wrappers on a clean work surface, spread 60 ml filling at the edge of each wrapper and leave a ½-inch edge uncovering. 3. Wet the edges of the wrappers with water and fold the uncovered edge over the filling. Fold the left and right sides in the centre, then tuck the edge under the filling and fold to wrap the filling. 4. Brush the wrappers with melted butter, then arrange the wrappers in a single layer in the preheated two air fryer drawers, seam side down. 5. Leave a little space between each two wrappers. Air fry for 10 minutes or until golden brown. 6. Serve immediately.

Easy Cinnamon Toast

1½ teaspoons cinnamon	pepper
1½ teaspoons vanilla extract	2 tablespoons melted coconut oil
120 ml sugar	
2 teaspoons ground black	12 slices wholemeal bread

1.Preheat the air fryer to 204℃. 2. Combine all the ingredients, except for the bread, in a large bowl. Stir to mix well. 3. Dunk the bread in the bowl of mixture gently to coat and infuse well. Shake the excess off. 4. Arrange the bread slices in the two preheated air fryer drawers. Air fry for 5 minutes or until golden brown. Flip the bread halfway through. 5. Remove the bread slices from the air fryer and slice to serve.

Frico and Garlicky Baked Cherry Tomatoes

Frico:	Tomatoes:
235 ml shredded aged Manchego cheese	475 ml cherry tomatoes
1 teaspoon plain flour	1 clove garlic, thinly sliced
½ teaspoon cumin seeds	1 teaspoon olive oil
¼ teaspoon cracked black pepper	⅛ teaspoon rock salt
	1 tablespoon freshly chopped basil, for topping
Garlicky Baked Cherry	Cooking spray

Make the Frico (zone 1 drawer): 1. Preheat the zone 1 air fryer drawer to 190℃. Line the zone 1 air fryer drawer with parchment paper. 2. Combine the cheese and flour in a bowl. Stir to mix well. Spread the mixture in the drawer into a 4-inch round. 3. Combine the cumin and black pepper in a small bowl. Stir to mix well. Sprinkle the cumin mixture over the cheese round. 4. Air fry 5 minutes or until the cheese is lightly browned and frothy. 5. Use tongs to transfer the cheese wafer onto a plate and slice to serve.
Make the Garlicky Baked Cherry Tomatoes (zone 2 drawer): 1. Preheat the zone 2 air fryer drawer to 180℃. 2. Spritz the air fryer baking pan with cooking spray and set aside. 3. In a large bowl, toss together the cherry tomatoes, sliced garlic, olive oil, and rock salt. Spread the mixture in an even layer in the prepared pan. 4. Bake in the preheated air fryer for 4 to 6 minutes, or until the tomatoes become soft and wilted. 5. Transfer to a bowl and rest for 5 minutes. 6. Top with the chopped basil and serve warm.

Golden Salmon and Carrot Croquettes

2 egg whites	2 tablespoons minced garlic cloves
235 ml almond flour	
235 ml panko breadcrumbs	120 ml chopped onion
450 g chopped salmon fillet	2 tablespoons chopped chives
160 ml grated carrots	Cooking spray

1.Preheat the zone 1 air fryer drawer to 176℃. 2. Spritz the zone 1 air fryer drawer with cooking spray. 3. Whisk the egg whites in a bowl. Put the flour in a second bowl. Pour the breadcrumbs in a third bowl. Set aside. Combine the salmon, carrots, garlic, onion, and chives in a large bowl. Stir to mix well. 4. Form the mixture into balls with your hands. Dredge the balls into the flour, then egg, and then breadcrumbs to coat well. 5. Arrange the salmon balls in the preheated air fryer and spritz with cooking spray. Air fry for 10 minutes or until crispy and browned. Shake the drawer halfway through. 6. Serve immediately.

Garlicky Zoodles

Prep time: 10 minutes | Cook time: 10 minutes | Serves 4

2 large courgette, peeled and spiralized	½ teaspoon rock salt
2 large yellow butternut squash, peeled and spiralized	1 garlic clove, whole
	2 tablespoons fresh basil, chopped
1 tablespoon olive oil, divided	Cooking spray

1.Preheat the air fryer to 182ºC. 2. Spritz the zone 1 air fryer drawer with cooking spray. Combine the courgette and butternut squash with 1 teaspoon olive oil and salt in a large bowl. Toss to coat well. 3. Transfer the courgette and butternut squash in the preheated air fryer and add the garlic. Air fry for 10 minutes or until tender and fragrant. Toss the spiralized courgette and butternut squash halfway through the cooking time. 4. Transfer the cooked courgette and butternut squash onto a plate and set aside. Remove the garlic from the air fryer and allow to cool for a few minutes. 5. Mince the garlic and combine with remaining olive oil in a small bowl. Stir to mix well. 6. Drizzle the spiralized courgette and butternut squash with garlic oil and sprinkle with basil. Toss to serve.

Easy Air Fried Edamame

Prep time: 5 minutes | Cook time: 7 minutes | Serves 6

680 g unshelled edamame	1 teaspoon sea salt
2 tablespoons olive oil	

1.Preheat the air fryer to 204ºC. 2. Place the edamame in a large bowl, then drizzle with olive oil. Toss to coat well. 3. Transfer the edamame to the two preheated air fryer drawers. Cook for 7 minutes or until tender and warmed through. Shake the drawers at least three times during the cooking. 4. Transfer the cooked edamame onto a plate and sprinkle with salt. 5. Toss to combine well and set aside for 3 minutes to infuse before serving.

Cinnamon Rolls with Cream Glaze

Prep time: 2 hours 15 minutes | Cook time: 10 minutes | Serves 8

450 g frozen bread dough, thawed	Cream Glaze:
	110 g soft white cheese
2 tablespoons melted butter	½ teaspoon vanilla extract
1½ tablespoons cinnamon	2 tablespoons melted butter
180 ml brown sugar	300 ml powdered erythritol
Cooking spray	

1.Place the bread dough on a clean work surface, then roll the dough out into a rectangle with a rolling pin. 2. Brush the top of the dough with melted butter and leave 1-inch edges uncovered. Combine the cinnamon and sugar in a small bowl, then sprinkle the dough with the cinnamon mixture. 3. Roll the dough over tightly, then cut the dough log into 8 portions. Wrap the portions in plastic, better separately, and let sit to rise for 1 or 2 hours. 4. Meanwhile, combine the ingredients for the glaze in a separate small bowl. Stir to mix well. Preheat the air fryer to 176ºC. 5. Spritz the two air fryer drawers with cooking spray. 6. Transfer the risen rolls to the preheated air fryer drawers. Air fry for 5 minutes or until golden brown. 7. Flip the rolls halfway through. Serve the rolls with the glaze.

Lemony and Garlicky Asparagus

Prep time: 5 minutes | Cook time: 10 minutes | Makes 10 spears

10 spears asparagus (about 230 g in total), snap the ends off	½ teaspoon salt
	¼ teaspoon ground black pepper
1 tablespoon lemon juice	
2 teaspoons minced garlic	Cooking spray

1.Preheat the zone 1 air fryer drawer to 204ºC. 2. Line a parchment paper in the zone 1 air fryer drawer. 3. Put the asparagus spears in a large bowl. Drizzle with lemon juice and sprinkle with minced garlic, salt, and ground black pepper. Toss to coat well. 4. Transfer the asparagus in the preheated air fryer and spritz with cooking spray. 5. Air fryer for 10 minutes or until wilted and soft. Flip the asparagus halfway through. 6. Serve immediately.

South Carolina Shrimp and Corn Bake

Prep time: 10 minutes | Cook time: 18 minutes | Serves 2

1 ear corn, husk and silk removed, cut into 2-inch rounds	pepper
	227 g large shrimps (about 12 shrimps), deveined
227 g red potatoes, unpeeled, cut into 1-inch pieces	170 g andouille or chorizo sausage, cut into 1-inch pieces
2 teaspoons Old Bay or all-purpose seasoning, divided	2 garlic cloves, minced
2 teaspoons vegetable oil, divided	1 tablespoon chopped fresh parsley
¼ teaspoon ground black	

1.Preheat the air fryer to 204ºC. 2. Put the corn rounds and potatoes in a large bowl. Sprinkle with 1 teaspoon of seasoning and drizzle with vegetable oil. Toss to coat well. 3. Transfer the corn rounds and potatoes on a baking sheet, then put in the preheated air fryer. Bake for 12 minutes or until soft and browned. Shake the drawer halfway through the cooking time. 4. Meanwhile, cut slits into the shrimps but be careful not to cut them through. Combine the shrimps, sausage, remaining seasoning, and remaining vegetable oil in the large bowl. Toss to coat well. 5. When the baking of the potatoes and corn rounds is complete, add the shrimps and sausage and bake for 6 more minutes or until the shrimps are opaque. Shake the drawer halfway through the cooking time. 6. When the baking is finished, serve them on a plate and spread with parsley before serving.

Air Fried Spicy Olives

Prep time: 10 minutes | Cook time: 5 minutes | Serves 4

340 g pitted black extra-large olives	1 teaspoon red pepper flakes
60 ml plain flour	1 teaspoon smoked paprika
235 ml panko breadcrumbs	1 egg beaten with 1 tablespoon water
2 teaspoons dried thyme	Vegetable oil for spraying

1.Preheat the air fryer to 204ºC. Drain the olives and place them on a paper towel–lined plate to dry. 2. Put the flour on a plate. Combine the panko, thyme, red pepper flakes, and paprika on a separate plate. Dip an olive in the flour, shaking off any excess, then coat with egg mixture. 3. Dredge the olive in the panko mixture, pressing to make the crumbs adhere, and place the breaded olive on a platter. 4. Repeat with the remaining olives. 5. Spray the olives with oil and place them in a single layer in the two air fryer drawers. Air fry for 5 minutes until the breading is browned and crispy. 6. Serve warm

Custard Donut Holes with Chocolate Glaze

Prep time: 1 hour 50 minutes | Cook time: 4 minutes | Makes 24 donut holes

Dough:	Custard Filling:
350 ml bread flour	1 (96 g) box French vanilla
2 egg yolks	instant pudding mix
1 teaspoon active dry yeast	60 ml double cream
120 ml warm milk	180 ml whole milk
½ teaspoon pure vanilla extract	Chocolate Glaze:
2 tablespoons butter, melted	80 ml double cream
1 tablespoon sugar	235 ml chocolate chips
¼ teaspoon salt	Special Equipment:
Cooking spray	A pastry bag with a long tip

1.Combine the ingredients for the dough in a food processor, then pulse until a satiny dough ball forms. 2. Transfer the dough on a lightly floured work surface, then knead for 2 minutes by hand and shape the dough back to a ball. 3. Spritz a large bowl with cooking spray, then transfer the dough ball into the bowl. Wrap the bowl in plastic and let it rise for 1½ hours or until it doubled in size. 4. Transfer the risen dough on a floured work surface, then shape it into a 24-inch-long log. Cut the log into 24 parts and shape each part into a ball. Transfer the balls on two or three baking sheets and let sit to rise for 30 more minutes. 5. Preheat the air fryer to 204ºC. Arrange the baking sheets in the two air fryer drawers. Spritz the balls with cooking spray. Bake for 4 minutes or until golden brown. Flip the balls halfway through. 6. Meanwhile, combine the ingredients for the filling in a large bowl and whisk for 2 minutes with a hand mixer until well combined. 7. Pour the double cream in a saucepan, then bring to a boil. Put the chocolate chips in a small bowl and pour in the boiled double cream immediately. 8. Mix until the chocolate chips are melted, and the mixture is smooth. 9. Transfer the baked donut holes to a large plate, then pierce a hole into each donut hole and lightly hollow them. Pour the filling in a pastry bag with a long tip and gently squeeze the filling into the donut holes. 10. Then top the donut holes with chocolate glaze. Allow to sit for 10 minutes, then serve.

Hasselback Potatoes

Prep time: 5 minutes | Cook time: 50 minutes | Serves 4

4 russet or Maris Piper potatoes, peeled	pepper, to taste
Salt and freshly ground black	60 ml grated Parmesan cheese
	Cooking spray

1.Preheat the air fryer to 204ºC. 2. Spray the zone 1 air fryer drawer lightly with cooking spray. 3. Make thin parallel cuts into each potato, ⅛-inch to ¼-inch apart, stopping at about ½ of the way through. The potato needs to stay intact along the bottom. 4. Spray the potatoes with cooking spray and use the hands or a silicone brush to completely coat the potatoes lightly in oil. 5. Put the potatoes, sliced side up, in the zone 1 air fryer drawer in a single layer. Leave a little room between each potato. Sprinkle the potatoes lightly with salt and black pepper. Air fry for 20 minutes. 6. Reposition the potatoes and spritz lightly with cooking spray again. Air fry until the potatoes are fork-tender and crispy and browned, another 20 to 30 minutes. 7. Sprinkle the potatoes with Parmesan cheese and serve.

Classic Latkes

Prep time: 15 minutes | Cook time: 10 minutes | Makes 4 latkes

1 egg	¼ teaspoon granulated garlic
2 tablespoons plain flour	½ teaspoon salt
2 medium potatoes, peeled and shredded, rinsed and drained	Cooking spray

1.Preheat the zone 1 air fryer drawer to 192ºC. 2. Spritz the zone 1 air fryer drawer with cooking spray. 3. Whisk together the egg, flour, potatoes, garlic, and salt in a large bowl. Stir to mix well. Divide the mixture into four parts, then flatten them into four circles. 4. Arrange the circles into the preheated air fryer. Spritz the circles with cooking spray, then air fry for 10 minutes or until golden brown and crispy. Flip the latkes halfway through. 5. Serve immediately.

Chapter 8 Desserts

Chapter 8 Desserts

Pumpkin-Spice Bread Pudding

Prep time: 15 minutes | Cook time: 35 minutes | Serves 6

Bread Pudding:
175 ml heavy whipping cream
120 g canned pumpkin
80 ml whole milk
65 g granulated sugar
1 large egg plus 1 yolk
½ teaspoon pumpkin pie spice
⅛ teaspoon kosher, or coarse
sea salt

1/3 loaf of day-old baguette or
crusty country bread, cubed
4 tablespoons unsalted butter,
melted
Sauce:
80 ml pure maple syrup
1 tablespoon unsalted butter
120 ml heavy whipping cream
½ teaspoon pure vanilla extract

1. For the bread pudding: In a medium bowl, combine the cream, pumpkin, milk, sugar, egg and yolk, pumpkin pie spice, and salt. Whisk until well combined. 2. In a large bowl, toss the bread cubes with the melted butter. Add the pumpkin mixture and gently toss until the ingredients are well combined. 3. Transfer the mixture to a baking pan. Place the pan in the zone 1 air fryer drawer. Set the temperature to 176°C cooking for 35 minutes, or until custard is set in the middle. 4. Meanwhile, for the sauce: In a small saucepan, combine the syrup and butter. Heat over medium heat, stirring, until the butter melts. Stir in the cream and simmer, stirring often, until the sauce has thickened, about 15 minutes. Stir in the vanilla. Remove the pudding from the air fryer. 5. Let the pudding stand for 10 minutes before serving with the warm sauce.

Grilled Pineapple and Mixed Berries with Pecan Streusel Topping

Prep time: 10 minutes | Cook time: 17 minutes | Serves 7

Grilled Pineapple:
Coconut, or avocado oil for
misting, or cooking spray
4½-inch-thick slices fresh
pineapple, core removed
1 tablespoon honey
¼ teaspoon brandy, or apple
juice
2 tablespoons slivered almonds,
toasted
Vanilla frozen yogurt, coconut
sorbet, or ice cream
Mixed Berries with Pecan

Streusel Topping:
75 g mixed berries
Cooking spray
Topping:
1 egg, beaten
3 tablespoons almonds, slivered
3 tablespoons chopped pecans
2 tablespoons chopped walnuts
3 tablespoons granulated
sweetener
2 tablespoons cold salted butter,
cut into pieces
½ teaspoon ground cinnamon

Make the Grilled Pineapple (zone 1 drawer): 1. Spray both sides of pineapple slices with oil or cooking spray. Place into the zone 1 air fryer drawer. 2. Air fry at 200°C for 6 minutes. Turn slices over and cook for an additional 6 minutes. 3. Mix together the honey and brandy. 4. Remove cooked pineapple slices from air fryer, sprinkle with toasted almonds, and drizzle with honey mixture. 5. Serve with a scoop of frozen yogurt or sorbet on the side.
Make the Mixed Berries with Pecan Streusel Topping (zone 2 drawer): 1. Preheat the zone 2 air fryer drawer to 172°C. Lightly spray a baking dish with cooking spray. 2. Make the topping: In a medium bowl, stir together the beaten egg, nuts, sweetener, butter, and cinnamon until well blended. 3. Put the mixed berries in the bottom of the baking dish and spread the topping over the top. 4. Bake in the preheated air fryer drawer for 17 minutes, or until the fruit is bubbly and topping is golden brown. 5. Allow to cool for 5 to 10 minutes before serving.

Berry Crumble and S'mores

Prep time: 15 minutes | Cook time: 15 minutes | Serves 8

Berry Crumble:
For the Filling:
300 g mixed berries
2 tablespoons sugar
1 tablespoon cornflour
1 tablespoon fresh lemon juice
For the Topping:
30 g plain flour
20 g rolled oats
1 tablespoon granulated sugar

2 tablespoons cold unsalted
butter, cut into small cubes
Whipped cream or ice cream
(optional)
S'mores:
Coconut, or avocado oil, for
spraying
8 digestive biscuits
2 (45 g) chocolate bars
4 large marshmallows

Make the Berry Crumble (zone 1 drawer): 1. Preheat the air fryer to 204°C. 2. For the filling: In a round baking pan, gently mix the berries, sugar, cornflour, and lemon juice until thoroughly combined. 3. For the topping: In a small bowl, combine the flour, oats, and sugar. Stir the butter into the flour mixture until the mixture has the consistency of breadcrumbs. 4. Sprinkle the topping over the berries. 5. Put the pan in the zone 1 air fryer drawer and air fry for 15 minutes. Let cool for 5 minutes on a wire rack. 6. Serve topped with whipped cream or ice cream, if desired.
Make the S'mores (zone 2 drawer): 1. Line the zone 2 air fryer drawer with baking paper and spray lightly with oil. 2. Place 4 biscuits into the prepared drawer. 3. Break the chocolate bars in half, and place 1/2 on top of each biscuit. Top with 1 marshmallow. 4. Air fry at 188°C for 30 seconds, or until the marshmallows are puffed, golden brown and slightly melted. 5. Top with the remaining biscuits and serve.

Glazed Cherry Turnovers

Prep time: 10 minutes | Cook time: 14 minutes | Serves 8

2 sheets frozen puff pastry, thawed
600 g can premium cherry pie filling
2 teaspoons ground cinnamon
1 egg, beaten
90 g sliced almonds
120 g icing sugar
2 tablespoons milk

1. Roll a sheet of puff pastry out into a square that is approximately 10-inches by 10-inches. Cut this large square into quarters. 2. Mix the cherry pie filling and cinnamon together in a bowl. Spoon ¼ cup of the cherry filling into the center of each puff pastry square. Brush the perimeter of the pastry square with the egg wash. Fold one corner of the puff pastry over the cherry pie filling towards the opposite corner, forming a triangle. Seal the two edges of the pastry together with the tip of a fork, making a design with the tines. Brush the top of the turnovers with the egg wash and sprinkle sliced almonds over each one. Repeat these steps with the second sheet of puff pastry. You should have eight turnovers at the end. 3. Preheat the air fryer to 188°C. 4. Air fry turnovers in the two drawers for 14 minutes, carefully turning them over halfway through the cooking time. 5. While the turnovers are cooking, make the glaze by whisking the icing sugar and milk together in a small bowl until smooth. Let the glaze sit for a minute so the sugar can absorb the milk. If the consistency is still too thick to drizzle, add a little more milk, a drop at a time, and stir until smooth. 6. Let the cooked cherry turnovers sit for at least 10 minutes. Then drizzle the glaze over each turnover in a zigzag motion. Serve warm or at room temperature.

Pineapple Wontons

Prep time: 15 minutes | Cook time: 15 to 18 minutes | Serves 5

225 g cream cheese
170 g finely chopped fresh pineapple
20 wonton wrappers
Cooking oil spray

1. In a small microwave-safe bowl, heat the cream cheese in the microwave on high power for 20 seconds to soften. 2. In a medium bowl, stir together the cream cheese and pineapple until mixed well. 3. Lay out the wonton wrappers on a work surface. A clean table or large cutting board works well. 4. Spoon 1½ teaspoons of the cream cheese mixture onto each wrapper. Be careful not to overfill. 5. Fold each wrapper diagonally across to form a triangle. Bring the 2 bottom corners up toward each other. Do not close the wrapper yet. Bring up the 2 open sides and push out any air. Squeeze the open edges together to seal. 6. Preheat the air fryer to 200°C. 7. Place the wontons into the two drawers. Spray the wontons with the cooking oil. 8. Cook wontons for 10 minutes, then remove the drawers, flip each wonton, and spray them with more oil. Reinsert the drawers to resume cooking for 5 to 8 minutes more until the wontons are light

golden brown and crisp. 9. When the cooking is complete, cool for 5 minutes before serving.

Butter and Chocolate Chip Cookies

Prep time: 20 minutes | Cook time: 11 minutes | Serves 8

110 g unsalted butter, at room temperature
155 g powdered sweetener
60 g chunky peanut butter
1 teaspoon vanilla paste
75 g coconut flour
35 g cocoa powder, unsweetened
1 ½ teaspoons baking powder
¼ teaspoon ground cinnamon
¼ teaspoon ginger
85 g unsweetened, or dark chocolate chips
1 fine almond flour

1. In a mixing dish, beat the butter and sweetener until creamy and uniform. Stir in the peanut butter and vanilla. 2. In another mixing dish, thoroughly combine the flour, cocoa powder, baking powder, cinnamon, and ginger. 3. Add the flour mixture to the peanut butter mixture; mix to combine well. Afterwards, fold in the chocolate chips. Drop by large spoonsful onto two baking paper-lined air fryer drawers. Bake at 185°C for 11 minutes or until golden brown on the top. Bon appétit!

Homemade Mint Pie and Strawberry Pecan Pie

Prep time: 30 minutes | Cook time: 25 minutes | Serves 8

Homemade Mint Pie:
1 tablespoon instant coffee
2 tablespoons almond butter, softened
2 tablespoons granulated sweetener
1 teaspoon dried mint
3 eggs, beaten
1 teaspoon dried spearmint
4 teaspoons coconut flour
Cooking spray
Strawberry Pecan Pie:
190 g whole shelled pecans
1 tablespoon unsalted butter, softened
240 ml heavy whipping cream
12 medium fresh strawberries, hulled
2 tablespoons sour cream

Make the Homemade Mint Pie: 1. Spray the zone 1 air fryer drawer with cooking spray. 2. Then mix all ingredients in the mixer bowl. 3. When you get a smooth mixture, transfer it in the zone 1 air fryer drawer. Flatten it gently. Cook the pie at 185°C for 25 minutes.
Make the Strawberry Pecan Pie: 1. Place pecans and butter into a food processor and pulse ten times until a dough forms. Press dough into the bottom of an ungreased round nonstick baking dish. 2. Place dish into the zone 2 air fryer drawer. Adjust the temperature to 160°C and set the timer for 10 minutes. Crust will be firm and golden when done. Let cool 20 minutes. 3. In a large bowl, whisk cream until fluffy and doubled in size, about 2 minutes. 4. In a separate large bowl, mash strawberries until mostly liquid. Fold strawberries and sour cream into whipped cream. 5. Spoon mixture into cooled crust, cover, and place in refrigerator for at least 30 minutes to set. Serve chilled.

Fried Cheesecake Bites

Prep time: 30 minutes | Cook time: 2 minutes | Makes 16 bites

225 g cream cheese, softened
50 g powdered sweetener, plus
2 tablespoons, divided
4 tablespoons heavy cream,
divided
½ teaspoon vanilla extract
50 g almond flour

1. In a stand mixer fitted with a paddle attachment, beat the cream cheese, 50 g of the sweetener, 2 tablespoons of the heavy cream, and the vanilla until smooth. Using a small ice-cream scoop, divide the mixture into 16 balls and arrange them on a rimmed baking sheet lined with baking paper. Freeze for 45 minutes until firm. 2. Line the two air fryer drawers with baking paper and preheat the air fryer to 176ºC. 3. In a small shallow bowl, combine the almond flour with the remaining 2 tablespoons of sweetener. 4. In another small shallow bowl, place the remaining 2 tablespoons cream. 5. One at a time, dip the frozen cheesecake balls into the cream and then roll in the almond flour mixture, pressing lightly to form an even coating. Arrange the balls in a single layer in the two air fryer drawers, leaving room between them. Air fry for 2 minutes until the coating is lightly browned.

Mini Peanut Butter Tarts

Prep time: 25 minutes | Cook time: 12 to 15 minutes | Serves 8

125 g pecans
110 g finely ground blanched almond flour
2 tablespoons unsalted butter, at room temperature
50 g powdered sweetener, plus
2 tablespoons, divided
120 g heavy (whipping) cream
2 tablespoons mascarpone
cheese
110 g cream cheese
140 g sugar-free peanut butter
1 teaspoon pure vanilla extract
⅛ teaspoon sea salt
85 g organic chocolate chips
1 tablespoon coconut oil
40 g chopped peanuts or pecans

1. Place the pecans in the bowl of a food processor; process until they are finely ground. 2. Transfer the ground pecans to a medium bowl and stir in the almond flour. Add the butter and 2 tablespoons of sweetener and stir until the mixture becomes wet and crumbly. 3. Divide the mixture among 8 silicone muffin cups, pressing the crust firmly with your fingers into the bottom and part way up the sides of each cup. 4. Arrange the muffin cups in the two air fryer drawers. Set the air fryer to 148ºC and bake for 12 to 15 minutes, until the crusts begin to brown. Remove the cups from the air fryer and set them aside to cool. 5. In the bowl of a stand mixer, combine the heavy cream and mascarpone cheese. Beat until peaks form. Transfer to a large bowl. 6. In the same stand mixer bowl, combine the cream cheese, peanut butter, remaining 50 g sweetener, vanilla, and salt. Beat at medium-high speed until smooth. 7. Reduce the speed to low and add the heavy cream mixture back a spoonful at a time, beating after each addition. 8. Spoon the peanut butter mixture over the crusts and freeze the tarts for 30 minutes. 9. Place the chocolate chips and coconut oil in the top of a double boiler over high heat. Stir until melted, then remove from the heat. 10. Drizzle the melted chocolate over the peanut butter tarts. Top with the chopped nuts and freeze the tarts for another 15 minutes, until set. 11. Store the peanut butter tarts in an airtight container in the refrigerator for up to 1 week or in the freezer for up to 1 month.

Zucchini Bread

Prep time: 10 minutes | Cook time: 40 minutes | Serves 12

220 g coconut flour
2 teaspoons baking powder
150 g granulated sweetener
120 ml coconut oil, melted
1 teaspoon apple cider vinegar
1 teaspoon vanilla extract
3 eggs, beaten
1 courgette, grated
1 teaspoon ground cinnamon

1. In the mixing bowl, mix coconut flour with baking powder, sweetener, coconut oil, apple cider vinegar, vanilla extract, eggs, courgette, and ground cinnamon. 2. Transfer the mixture into the two air fryer drawers and flatten it in the shape of the bread. 3. Cook the bread at 176ºC for 40 minutes.

Simple Pineapple Sticks and Crispy Pineapple Rings

Prep time: 10 minutes | Cook time: 10 minutes | Serves 9

Simple Pineapple Sticks:
½ fresh pineapple, cut into sticks
25 g desiccated coconut
Crispy Pineapple Rings:
240 ml rice milk
85 g plain flour
120 ml water
25 g unsweetened flaked coconut
4 tablespoons granulated sugar
½ teaspoon baking soda
½ teaspoon baking powder
½ teaspoon vanilla essence
½ teaspoon ground cinnamon
¼ teaspoon ground star anise
Pinch of kosher, or coarse sea salt
1 medium pineapple, peeled and sliced

Simple Pineapple Sticks (zone 1 drawer): 1. Preheat the air fryer to 204ºC. 2. Coat the pineapple sticks in the desiccated coconut and put in the zone 1 air fryer drawer. 3. Air fry for 10 minutes. 4. Serve immediately

Crispy Pineapple Rings (zone 2 drawer): 1. Preheat the air fryer to 204ºC. 2. In a large bowl, stir together all the ingredients except the pineapple. 3. Dip each pineapple slice into the batter until evenly coated. 4. Arrange the pineapple slices in the zone 2 drawer and air fry for 6 to 8 minutes until golden brown. 5. Remove from the drawer to a plate and cool for 5 minutes before serving warm

Crustless Peanut Butter Cheesecake and Pumpkin Pudding with Vanilla Wafers

Prep time: 20 minutes | Cook time: 17 minutes | Serves 6

Crustless Peanut Butter
Cheesecake:
110 g cream cheese, softened
2 tablespoons powdered
sweetener
1 tablespoon all-natural, no-
sugar-added peanut butter
½ teaspoon vanilla extract
1 large egg, whisked
Pumpkin Pudding with Vanilla
Wafers:
250 g canned no-salt-added

pumpkin purée (not pumpkin
pie filling)
50 g packed brown sugar
3 tablespoons plain flour
1 egg, whisked
2 tablespoons milk
1 tablespoon unsalted butter,
melted
1 teaspoon pure vanilla extract
4 low-fat vanilla, or plain
wafers, crumbled
Nonstick cooking spray

Make the Crustless Peanut Butter Cheesecake (zone 1 drawer): 1. In a medium bowl, mix cream cheese and sweetener until smooth. Add peanut butter and vanilla, mixing until smooth. Add egg and stir just until combined. 2. Spoon mixture into an ungreased springform pan and place into the zone 1 air fryer drawer. Adjust the temperature to 148°C and bake for 10 minutes. Edges will be firm, but center will be mostly set with only a small amount of jiggle when done. 3. Let pan cool at room temperature 30 minutes, cover with plastic wrap, then place into refrigerator at least 2 hours. Serve chilled.
Make the Pumpkin Pudding with Vanilla Wafers (zone 2 drawer): 1. Preheat the air fryer to 176°C. Coat a baking pan with nonstick cooking spray. Set aside. 2. Mix the pumpkin purée, brown sugar, flour, whisked egg, milk, melted butter, and vanilla in a medium bowl and whisk to combine. Transfer the mixture to the baking pan. 3. Place the baking pan in the zone 2 air fryer drawer and bake for 12 to 17 minutes until set. 4. Remove the pudding from the drawer to a wire rack to cool. 5. Divide the pudding into four bowls and serve with the vanilla wafers sprinkled on top.

Baked Brazilian Pineapple

Prep time: 10 minutes | Cook time: 10 minutes | Serves 4

95 g brown sugar
2 teaspoons ground cinnamon
1 small pineapple, peeled,

cored, and cut into spears
3 tablespoons unsalted butter,
melted

1. In a small bowl, mix the brown sugar and cinnamon until thoroughly combined. 2. Brush the pineapple spears with the melted butter. Sprinkle the cinnamon-sugar over the spears, pressing lightly to ensure it adheres well. 3. Place the spears in the two air fryer drawers in a single layer. Set the air fryer to 204°C and cook for 10 minutes. Halfway through the cooking time, brush the spears with butter. 4. The pineapple spears are done when they are heated through, and the sugar is bubbling. Serve hot.

Apple Wedges with Apricots and Coconut Mixed Berry Crisp

Prep time: 10 minutes | Cook time: 20 minutes |
Serves 10

Apple Wedges with Apricots:
4 large apples, peeled and sliced
into 8 wedges
2 tablespoons light olive oil
95 g dried apricots, chopped
1 to 2 tablespoons granulated
sugar
½ teaspoon ground cinnamon
Coconut Mixed Berry Crisp:

1 tablespoon butter, melted
340 g mixed berries
65 g granulated sweetener
1 teaspoon pure vanilla extract
½ teaspoon ground cinnamon
¼ teaspoon ground cloves
¼ teaspoon grated nutmeg
50 g coconut chips, for garnish

Make the Apple Wedges with Apricots (zone 1 drawer): 1. Preheat the zone 1 air fryer drawer to 180°C. 2. Toss the apple wedges with the olive oil in a mixing bowl until well coated. 3. Place the apple wedges in the zone 1 air fryer drawer and air fry for 12 to 15 minutes. 4. Sprinkle with the dried apricots and air fry for another 3 minutes. 5. Meanwhile, thoroughly combine the sugar and cinnamon in a small bowl. 6. Remove the apple wedges from the drawer to a plate. Serve sprinkled with the sugar mixture.
Make the Coconut Mixed Berry Crisp (zone 2 drawer): 1. Preheat the zone 2 air fryer drawer to 164°C. Coat a baking pan with melted butter. 2. Put the remaining ingredients except the coconut chips in the prepared baking pan. 3. Bake in the preheated air fryer for 20 minutes. 4. Serve garnished with the coconut chips.

Funnel Cake

Prep time: 10 minutes | Cook time: 5 minutes | Serves 4

Coconut, or avocado oil, for
spraying
110 g self-raising flour, plus
more for dusting

240 ml fat-free vanilla Greek
yogurt
½ teaspoon ground cinnamon
¼ cup icing sugar

1. Preheat the air fryer to 192°C. Line the two air fryer drawers with baking paper, and spray lightly with oil. 2. In a large bowl, mix together the flour, yogurt and cinnamon until the mixture forms a ball. 3. Place the dough on a lightly floured work surface and knead for about 2 minutes. 4. Cut the dough into 4 equal pieces, then cut each of those into 6 pieces. You should have 24 pieces in total. 5. Roll the pieces into 8- to 10-inch-long ropes. Loosely mound the ropes into 4 piles of 6 ropes. 6. Place the dough piles in the two prepared drawers, and spray liberally with oil. 7. Cook for 5 minutes, or until lightly browned. 8. Dust with the icing sugar before serving.

Maple-Pecan Tart with Sea Salt

Prep time: 15 minutes | Cook time: 25 minutes | Serves 8

Tart Crust:	4 tablespoons unsalted butter,
Vegetable oil spray	diced
75 g unsalted butter, softened	95 g packed brown sugar
50 g firmly packed brown sugar	60 ml pure maple syrup
125 g plain flour	60 ml whole milk
¼ teaspoon kosher, or coarse	¼ teaspoon pure vanilla extract
sea salt	190 g finely chopped pecans
Filling:	¼ teaspoon flaked sea salt

1. For the crust: Line a baking pan with foil, leaving a couple of inches of overhang. Spray the foil with vegetable oil spray. 2. In a medium bowl, combine the butter and brown sugar. Beat with an electric mixer on medium-low speed until light and fluffy. Add the flour and kosher salt and beat until the ingredients are well blended. Transfer the mixture (it will be crumbly) to the prepared pan. Press it evenly into the bottom of the pan. 3. Place the pan in the zone 1 air fryer drawer. Set the temperature to 176°C and cook for 13 minutes. When the crust has 5 minutes left to cook, start the filling. 4. For the filling: In a medium saucepan, combine the butter, brown sugar, maple syrup, and milk. Bring to a simmer, stirring occasionally. When it begins simmering, cook for 1 minute. Remove from the heat and stir in the vanilla and pecans. 5. Carefully pour the filling evenly over the crust, gently spreading with a rubber spatula so the nuts and liquid are evenly distributed. Keep the air fryer at 176°C and cook for 12 minutes, or until mixture is bubbling. (The center should still be slightly jiggly; it will thicken as it cools.) 6. Remove the pan from the air fryer and sprinkle the tart with the sea salt. Cool completely on a wire rack until room temperature. 7. Transfer the pan to the refrigerator to chill. When cold (the tart will be easier to cut), use the foil overhang to remove the tart from the pan and cut into 8 wedges. Serve at room temperature.

Spiced Apple Cake

Prep time: 15 minutes | Cook time: 30 minutes | Serves 6

Vegetable oil	1 tablespoon apple pie spice
2 diced & peeled Gala apples	½ teaspoon ground ginger
1 tablespoon fresh lemon juice	¼ teaspoon ground cardamom
55 g unsalted butter, softened	¼ teaspoon ground nutmeg
65 g granulated sugar	½ teaspoon kosher, or coarse
2 large eggs	sea salt
155 g plain flour	60 ml whole milk
1½ teaspoons baking powder	Icing sugar, for dusting

1. Grease a 0.7-liter Bundt, or tube pan with oil; set aside. 2. In a medium bowl, toss the apples with the lemon juice until well coated; set aside. 3. In a large bowl, combine the butter and sugar. Beat with an electric hand mixer on medium speed until the sugar has dissolved. Add the eggs and beat until fluffy. Add the flour, baking powder, apple pie spice, ginger, cardamom, nutmeg, salt, and milk. Mix until the batter is thick but pourable. 4. Pour the batter into the prepared pan. Top batter evenly with the apple mixture. Place the pan in the zone 1 air fryer drawer. Set the temperature to 176°C and cook for 30 minutes, or until a toothpick inserted in the center of the cake comes out clean. Close the air fryer and let the cake rest for 10 minutes. Turn the cake out onto a wire rack and cool completely. 5. Right before serving, dust the cake with icing sugar.

Lemon Raspberry Muffins

Prep time: 5 minutes | Cook time: 15 minutes | Serves 6

220 g almond flour	¼ teaspoon salt
75 g powdered sweetener	2 eggs
1¼ teaspoons baking powder	240 ml sour cream
⅓ teaspoon ground allspice	120 ml coconut oil
⅓ teaspoon ground star anise	60 g raspberries
½ teaspoon grated lemon zest	

1. Preheat the air fryer to 176°C. Line a muffin pan with 6 paper cases. 2. In a mixing bowl, mix the almond flour, sweetener, baking powder, allspice, star anise, lemon zest, and salt. 3. In another mixing bowl, beat the eggs, sour cream, and coconut oil until well mixed. Add the egg mixture to the flour mixture and stir to combine. Mix in the raspberries. 4. Scrape the batter into the prepared muffin cups, filling each about three-quarters full. 5. Bake for 15 minutes, or until the tops are golden and a toothpick inserted in the middle comes out clean. 6. Allow the muffins to cool for 10 minutes in the muffin pan before removing and serving.

Almond Shortbread

Prep time: 10 minutes | Cook time: 12 minutes | Serves 8

110 g unsalted butter	1 teaspoon pure almond extract
100 g granulated sugar	125 g plain flour

1. In bowl of a stand mixer fitted with the paddle attachment, beat the butter and sugar on medium speed until light and fluffy (3 to 4 minutes). Add the almond extract and beat until combined (about 30 seconds). Turn the mixer to low. Add the flour a little at a time and beat for about 2 minutes more until well-incorporated. 2. Pat the dough into an even layer in a baking pan. Place the pan in the zone 1 air fryer drawer. Set the air fryer to 192°C and bake for 12 minutes. 3. Carefully remove the pan from air fryer drawer. While the shortbread is still warm and soft, cut it into 8 wedges. 4. Let cool in the pan on a wire rack for 5 minutes. Remove the wedges from the pan and let cool completely on the rack before serving.

Lime Bars

Prep time: 10 minutes | Cook time: 33 minutes |
Makes 12 bars

140 g blanched finely ground almond flour, divided	4 tablespoons salted butter, melted
75 g powdered sweetener, divided	120 ml fresh lime juice
	2 large eggs, whisked

1. In a medium bowl, mix together 110 g flour, 25 g sweetener, and butter. Press mixture into bottom of an ungreased round nonstick cake pan. 2. Place pan into the zone 1 air fryer drawer. Adjust the temperature to 148°C and bake for 13 minutes. Crust will be brown and set in the middle when done. 3. Allow to cool in pan 10 minutes. 4. In a medium bowl, combine remaining flour, remaining sweetener, lime juice, and eggs. Pour mixture over cooled crust and return to air fryer for 20 minutes. Top will be browned and firm when done. 5. Let cool completely in pan, about 30 minutes, then chill covered in the refrigerator 1 hour. Serve chilled.

Coconut-Custard Pie and Pecan Brownies

Prep time: 20 minutes | Cook time: 20 to 23 minutes
| Serves 9

Coconut-Custard Pie:	50 g blanched finely ground almond flour
240 ml milk	
50 g granulated sugar, plus 2 tablespoons	55 g powdered sweetener
30 g scone mix	2 tablespoons unsweetened cocoa powder
1 teaspoon vanilla extract	½ teaspoon baking powder
2 eggs	55 g unsalted butter, softened
2 tablespoons melted butter	1 large egg
Cooking spray	35 g chopped pecans
50 g desiccated, sweetened coconut	40 g low-carb, sugar-free chocolate chips
Pecan Brownies:	

Make the Coconut-Custard Pie (zone 1 drawer): 1. Place all ingredients except coconut in a medium bowl. 2. Using a hand mixer, beat on high speed for 3 minutes. 3. Let sit for 5 minutes. 4. Preheat the air fryer to 164°C. 5. Spray a baking pan with cooking spray and place pan in the zone 1 air fryer drawer. 6. Pour filling into pan and sprinkle coconut over top. 7. Cook pie for 20 to 23 minutes or until center sets.

Make the Pecan Brownies (zone 2 drawer): 1. In a large bowl, mix almond flour, sweetener, cocoa powder, and baking powder. Stir in butter and egg. 2. Fold in pecans and chocolate chips. Scoop mixture into a round baking pan. Place pan into the zone 2 air fryer drawer. 3. Adjust the temperature to 148°C and bake for 20 minutes. 4. When fully cooked a toothpick inserted in center will come out clean. Allow 20 minutes to fully cool and firm up.

Bourbon Bread Pudding and Ricotta Lemon Poppy Seed Cake

Prep time: 20 minutes | Cook time: 55 minutes | Serves 8

Bourbon Bread Pudding :	Unsalted butter, at room temperature
3 slices whole grain bread, cubed	110 g almond flour
1 large egg	100 g granulated sugar
240 ml whole milk	3 large eggs
2 tablespoons bourbon, or peach juice	55 g heavy cream
½ teaspoons vanilla extract	60 g full-fat ricotta cheese
4 tablespoons maple syrup, divided	55 g coconut oil, melted
½ teaspoons ground cinnamon	2 tablespoons poppy seeds
2 teaspoons sparkling sugar	1 teaspoon baking powder
Ricotta Lemon Poppy Seed Cake:	1 teaspoon pure lemon extract
	Grated zest and juice of 1 lemon, plus more zest for garnish

Make the Bourbon Bread Pudding (zone 1 drawer): 1. Preheat the zone 1 air fryer drawer to 135°C. 2. Spray a baking pan with nonstick cooking spray, then place the bread cubes in the pan. 3. In a medium bowl, whisk together the egg, milk, bourbon, vanilla extract, 3 tablespoons of maple syrup, and cinnamon. Pour the egg mixture over the bread and press down with a spatula to coat all the bread, then sprinkle the sparkling sugar on top and bake for 20 minutes in the zone 1 drawer. 4. Remove the pudding from the air fryer and allow to cool in the pan on a wire rack for 10 minutes. Drizzle the remaining 1 tablespoon of maple syrup on top. Slice and serve warm.

Make the Ricotta Lemon Poppy Seed Cake (zone 2 drawer): 1. Generously butter a baking pan. Line the bottom of the pan with baking paper cut to fit. 2. In a large bowl, combine the almond flour, sugar, eggs, cream, ricotta, coconut oil, poppy seeds, baking powder, lemon extract, lemon zest, and lemon juice. Beat with a hand mixer on medium speed, until well blended and fluffy. 3. Pour the batter into the prepared pan. Cover the pan tightly with aluminum foil. Set the pan in the zone 2 air fryer drawer. Set the temperature to 164°C and cook for 45 minutes. Remove the foil and cook for 10 to 15 minutes more, until a knife (do not use a toothpick) inserted into the center of the cake comes out clean. 4. Let the cake cool in the pan on a wire rack for 10 minutes. Remove the cake from pan and let it cool on the rack for 15 minutes before slicing. 5. Top with additional lemon zest, slice and serve.

Caramelized Fruit Skewers

Prep time: 10 minutes | Cook time: 3 to 5 minutes | Serves 4

2 peaches, peeled, pitted, and thickly sliced
3 plums, halved and pitted
3 nectarines, halved and pitted
1 tablespoon honey
½ teaspoon ground cinnamon

¼ teaspoon ground allspice
Pinch cayenne pepper
Special Equipment:
8 metal skewers

1. Preheat the air fryer to 204°C. 2. Thread, alternating peaches, plums, and nectarines, onto the metal skewers that fit into the air fryer. 3. Thoroughly combine the honey, cinnamon, allspice, and cayenne in a small bowl. Brush the glaze generously over the fruit skewers. 4. Transfer the fruit skewers to the two air fryer drawers. 5. Air fry for 3 to 5 minutes, or until the fruit is caramelized. 6. Remove from the drawers. 7. Let the fruit skewers rest for 5 minutes before serving.

Printed in Great Britain
by Amazon